PENGUIN BC

THE ESSENTIAL GO...

Maria Teresa (Tessa) was born in Mu... ... She graduated from St. Xavier's College and soon a... married an officer in the Indian Navy. Her father, as Honorary Counsel for Brazil, would often entertain at home, with one of the daughters being made responsible for the menu and overseeing the cooking. The cuisine was normally Goan. Tessa's mother-in-law, Maria Felicia Menezes, was also an excellent cook. A lot of the recipes in this book are a result of watching Maria Felicia in the kitchen and noting down the ingredients.

Although she has travelled widely and now lives in Pune, Tessa's heart is very much in Goa.

THE ESSENTIAL GOA COOKBOOK

Maria Teresa Menezes

Illustrations by Mario de Miranda

PENGUIN BOOKS

PENGUIN BOOKS

USA | Canada | UK | Ireland | Australia
New Zealand | India | South Africa | China

Penguin Books is part of the Penguin Random House group of companies
whose addresses can be found at global.penguinrandomhouse.com

Published by Penguin Random House India Pvt. Ltd
7th Floor, Infinity Tower C, DLF Cyber City,
Gurgaon 122 002, Haryana, India

First published by Penguin Books India 2000

Copyright © Maria Teresa Menezes 2000

Series Editor: Bhicoo J. Manekshaw

18 17 16 15 14 13

ISBN 9780141000879

Typeset in Sabon by Digital Technologies and Printing Solutions, New Delhi
Printed at Repro Knowledgecast Limited, Thane

www.penguinbooksindia.com

To Henry
without whose encouragement my repertoire might have
been confined to fish curry and sorpotel. He was my
chief mentor and taster, and his appreciation spurred me
on to try new recipes and innovations, most of which
appear in this book.

Contents

Acknowledgements   ix

Foreword   x

Introduction   1

Appetizers   49

Soups   75

Fish   87

Chicken   137

Mutton and Beef   155

Pork   187

Vegetables   219

Rice   249

Breads   259

Desserts   271

Sweets   293

Relishes, Chutneys and Pickles   325
Beverages   349

Glossary   356
References   360
Index   361

Acknowledgements

But for my son Larry this book would never have been written—so, with love, my first thanks go to him, himself no mean gourmet chef.

My daughter Sherry patiently typed, advised and corrected, somehow deciphering my atrocious scrawl—I thank her too, with love.

I thank all my good friends who generously gave me their advice and their family recipes. Among others:

Tatiana Pais, who keeps a true 'Pride of Goa' table.

Marie Elsa Lobo, Anita Viegas, Ida Noronha, who suggested and gave me such interesting recipes, and Flavia Ribeiro who helped with the Portuguese translations.

I want to thank Mario Miranda for so generously allowing the use of his famous cartoons.

My grateful thanks to Sherna Wadia who brought order and structure to the book.

A host of others have contributed wittingly or unwittingly with insights and anecdotes. I have tried to recognize them in the narrative and recipes, and I thank them all most sincerely.

Foreword

Maria Teresa Menezes was born on 7 March 1926. She was the twelfth of thirteen children born to her mother. She completed her education at the Fort Convent and St. Xavier's College, Mumbai where she got her Bachelor's degree in English Honours. Fourteen years later, much after her marriage, she went back to college to get her Bachelor's degree in Education. She has always been fond of writing and has won many prizes in English Language and Literature.

Her interest in cooking was initiated by her mother very early in life. Each of the eight daughters took it in turn to handle the kitchen for a month at a time.

Straight from college to the altar, she married the late Henry Menezes, an officer in the Indian Navy. Being married to a Service officer meant that she travelled far and wide and had to do a lot of entertaining.

She has created many dishes, one of them being Coconut Velvet, and has passed on her passion for cooking to her son Larry and daughter Sherry.

Tessa, as she is fondly called, is a warm and charming

person, typical of her delightful community. Her refreshing personality comes out in her writing.

The Essential Goa Cookbook is far more than a collection of recipes. It is a celebration of the lifestyle of the Goans and their magnificent cuisine.

Bhicoo J. Manekshaw
Series Editor

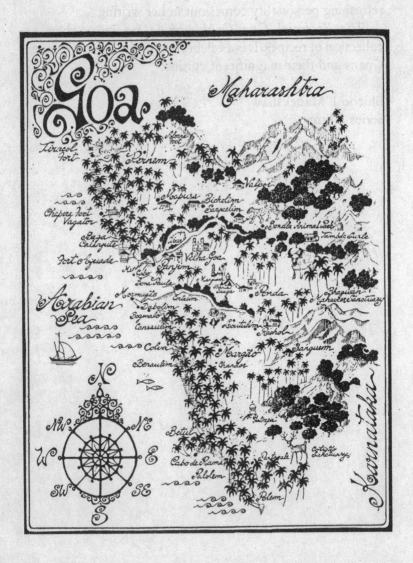

Introduction

Nostalgic memories of holidays spent in Goa during my early childhood first prompted me to record those halcyon days—to share those memories as a sort of legacy for my grandchildren. They had never known that era, nor the affectionate warmth of large family gatherings in vast mansions, where devoted family retainers cheerfully looked after everyone and produced an unending stream of food—both classic cuisine and good old soul food.

How clearly I recall the voyage by steamboat from Bombay to Panjim; the slow progress upriver to Divar in a flat-bottomed pathmari which was the sailing boat used along the coast; the creak of the oarlocks; the smell of tar; and the thrill of seeing shewto (mullet) arch out of the river in a silvery shimmering spray. From the landing on the island a box-like bullock-cart bounced us up the road to the house where my granduncle, Tio Julio, waited to welcome us home. In the kitchen, the caretaker/cook, dear old Quiteria, would be putting the finishing touches to lunch.

No matter that we children had been eating non-stop all the way from Bombay, the sea air and the holiday mood always sharpened our appetites, and we would go through the meal as though starving! First, a chicken soup with a hint of olive oil and alphabet macaroni in it, then croquettes with tambadi bhaji (red amaranthus) followed by prawn curry and Goa rice accompanied by a platter of small fried fish, netted at the sluice gate that very morning. Of course, it being May, bowls of mangoes ended the meal. Such menus were standard in most homes. For dinner, the rice and curry could be left out and a pudding or sweet replace the mangoes. Tea at 4 o'clock meant the various sweets we loved—merenda or a slice of doce, our favourite being doce de grao, made of Bengal gram, coconut and sugar—we particularly loved its soft sweetness.

May saw all the family assembled to celebrate the village feast in a relative's home—married sons and daughters, cousins and relatives, about thirty adults and twenty children. They brought maids and attendants with them and the cavernous kitchen with a battery of chulhas (cooking fires) at either end, would throb with activity. The wide kitchen veranda which gave out onto the backyard was furnished with four huge grinding stones of the pestle and mortar type, plus two sil-batti stones, which are flat grinding stones with rollers. Separate grinding stones were reserved for grinding the masalas for fish curries, meat curries, coconuts used in sweets, wet and dry masalas and masalas that did not require coconut. The sil-batti were backups for occasions when the house was really full! About fifteen to twenty coconuts were ground daily for various dishes, sweet and savoury, to feed family and attendants. Two fish curries, one mild and the other piquant, which were mandatory, plus fried fish of some sort, a meat entree and a couple of vegetables were the norm. The matriarch of the house—a delicate, exquisitely dressed lady, around seventy years old, would not come to table unless there were a specified number of dishes, nor would she take tea unless two sweet dishes were offered. It was not greed, but maintaining a way of life in which the appreciation of good food played an important part. Each recipe was meticulously followed. Tia Carolina who presided over the kitchen had amazingly sensitive taste buds.

A much later memory is that of the few days my husband and I with our two children spent with his cousin in Panjim, just after Liberation in 1961. It was a gracious villa built on the crest of the Altinho. The drawing-room or sala, exquisite with chandeliers and chinoiserie, overlooked the Mandovi river, while the spacious dining-room with a table to seat fourteen, looked towards the Zuari river, across fields of green paddy far below.

The old lifestyle persisted. We had coffee with small crisp loaves warm from the baker's, redolent with the toddy used as leaven, for breakfast. Lunch started with a creamy soup served with grated cheese, followed by slices of rawas (salmon) cooked with Portuguese olive oil and Goa palm vinegar. Next came assado, a lightly spiced roast beef, and then, mercifully, a plain boiled rice with a spicy prawn curry accompanied by thin slices of fried surmai (kingfish). Dessert was crème caramel, a favourite sweet in Goa. The host had an impressive cellar and Granjo and Tinto, the Portuguese white and red wines, were generously poured into the wineglasses. The conversation never lagged, we had so many years of separation to bridge.

That evening we returned from a visit to the beach to a

formal dinner hosted by another cousin. Fortunately, we had had a brisk walk on the sands and so could do justice to the food, which was exquisitely cooked and expertly served. Interestingly, before dinner, the women drank sherry but many of the men spurned Scotch for feni (the local cashew liquor)! That night we enjoyed consommé with vegetables julienne, a large fish with prawns, galantine of chicken, roast suckling pig with stuffing, arroz or rice with Goa sausages, and what nearly floored us, a magnificent bebinca, the classic forty-egg, twenty-layered cake itself! Each layer took thirty minutes to cook, the degchi or pan set on glowing embers with slow-burning coconut husks on the lid, each layer translucent with ghee (clarified butter), and golden brown on top.

Such a menu was almost standard for a formal dinner in those days. Since this dinner was a celebration of a family reunion, one of the cousins first became fidgety, then shot glances up and down the table, and finally jumped to his feet and burst into a speech in Portuguese and Konkani. Goans love making speeches—always emotional, full of involved sentences and flowery phrases, accompanied by highly dramatic gestures and postures.

One such speech comes to mind across the decades. My elder sister married in Goa in 1935, and the father of the bridegroom spared no expense to make the wedding of his eldest son memorable in every way—indeed, people talked about it for months after. To accommodate the five hundred or so guests, and in the absence of an adequate hall, a nearby field was levelled, and a circular matto or pandal (marquee) erected. It was divided into concentric circles with low 'fences' of matting. The outermost circle set with chairs and tables seated the guests, the inner circle was especially levelled for dancing, and the band sat on a raised platform in the centre. A generator had been installed, coloured lights and lanterns shone on the splendid dresses and jewellery of the women and the black tailcoats of the men—Portuguese influence was very evident in those days. Waiters offered trays of champagne and cake and a very distinguished gentleman prepared to raise the toast to the bridal couple.

As an eight-year-old child, I was fascinated, I remember, by his swept-back hair, his George V beard, his voice ringing out in the hushed matto, for he was a well-known orator, his coattails flying as he made sudden half-turns this way and that, arms out-flung! I am almost certain he rose on his toes in his enthusiasm, then sank back as applause greeted a particularly well-phrased passage. The speech, in flawless high-flown Portuguese, was laced with pithy Konkani phrases, because some things just cannot be expressed accurately in any other language.

After the bridegroom's reply, a constant stream of waiters offered refreshments. Trays of wines, liquors, the special xaropes or syrups of Goa (the almond flavoured orchata, brindão made from a sour plum called kokum, and the lime flavoured limão); and the most delectable canapés imaginable—light-as-air oyster patties, melt-in-the-mouth prawn rissóis or turnovers, delicately flavoured croquettes, tiny sausages, green and black olives, were served in an endless procession. We children concentrated on orchata, and of course, sampled every tray that passed us! Alas, we were shepherded to bed before the banquet was announced, but we did watch the bridal mando (the traditional Goan wedding folk song and dance) being danced with graceful dignity. The ladies stepping forwards and backwards with their fans fluttering, the gentlemen matching their steps, with hands behind their backs and heads held high. Western dance music was played throughout the evening, but the announcement of the bridal mando brought every man and woman onto the floor. For a Goan, no western music could ever equal the magic of the mando.

Another childhood memory is of a tea enjoyed at the home of a close family friend. Led into the dining room, we children looked with amazed delight at a table laden with bols (cakes), rissóis, guardanapos (pancakes soaked in coconut-jaggery syrup), dedos de dama (marzipan fingers coated with burnt sugar—literally meaning 'lady's fingers' in Portuguese) and of course crème caramel. It was a tour de force on the part of the cook who was determined to uphold the high reputation of the house.

The Beginning

Goans have migrated to almost every country, always carrying with them their warmth and hospitality, pride of family and a certain passion for excellence that is their special hallmark. My father a doctor, migrated to Bombay in the early part of the last century. In 1924, he was appointed honorary consul for Brazil. This meant joining the equivalent of the cocktail circuit of those days, and my parents had to host the occasional formal dinner. I clearly recall one such dinner. About ten to twelve guests were seated at the long dining table and enjoyed an elegant menu of:

Cream of Almond Soup
Rolled Fillet of Sole
Galantine of Chicken
Xacuti of Mutton
Leitria
Bebinca.

On such occasions, my mother would bring out her fine linen, crockery and glassware, some of it heirloom. In doing this, she maintained the lifestyle of the ancestral home in Goa.

This is a book about a little known cuisine, that of Goa. It is a cuisine intriguingly different from any other Indian cuisine, perhaps because of the European look and taste of some dishes, perhaps because of the sometimes-generous addition of toddy and feni. The Europeans themselves would declare that while the dishes looked and tasted European, there was a je ne sais quoi that made them Indian, and the Indians would say that the dishes made with local ingredients tasted different, not quite Indian. Both were right—the cuisine is authentic Goan.

It appears that the Portuguese longed for the pies, roasts, cakes and breads of home and ordered their Goan cooks to produce them with whatever was available locally. The Goans, themselves epicures, set to work with a will. The result was that the fish and meat pies were zested with slit green chillies, assado or roast was translated into the cuisine by marinating the meat with masala, pao or bread was fermented with toddy and the famous bol was made with coconut and semolina. In their enthusiasm, the cooks cured ham in feni, produced fruit leathers from jackfruit and mango by drying the pulp on banana leaves and substituted cashew nuts for almonds in a delectable marzipan.

Of the many colonial enclaves in India, it is only in Goa that a distinctive cuisine evolved and the process of evolution makes interesting reading for the dedicated gourmet. To appreciate the food-style, one needs to know something of the people, their history and the customs that helped shape the Goan identity and cuisine.

The visitor to Goa is struck by the geniality of the people. They are courteous and hospitable, appear well content with life, not driven by modern demons, in a word, they are sossegado—laid-back rather than lazy. They will work at a task at their own pace and do it well, whether it is stitching a suit of clothes, or building a house. The men can be deferential, but never servile, and the women have an air of cool self-confidence and natural dignity—but if the visitor attributes these characteristics solely to the 'civilising' effects of 450 years of Portuguese influence, he is sadly off the mark.

'Contrary to their experiences in Africa and Brazil, the Portuguese were confronted in Goa by an ancient culture with a very hierarchical social structure and customs defined by strict rules', observes Helder Carita in his book *Palaces of Goa.*

It was a culture more ancient than Hinduism. It was only when the first Hindu migrants came to Goa from over the ghats centuries ago, that the Goans adopted Hinduism.

'Goa's cultural wealth lies in its civilized conformism, in its belief that one must accept what one cannot possibly change, like history and its upheavals', says Mario Cabral e Sa in his book *Goã*.

To understand the people, one has to travel back through the mists of time and the many legends about the origins of this beautiful land, once known as Aparanta (A land beyond time). Geologists know that centuries ago the sea receded leaving a sandbank that soon developed into a verdant land, tucked between the mountains of the Western Ghats and the Arabian Sea. One charming legend has it that Lord Parusaram shot an arrow into the sea, which receded to reveal the fertile land where he and his family settled. They called the land Gomantak.

Gods aside, a Portuguese sea captain of the 16th century commented, 'The Island of Goa is so old a place that one finds nothing in the writings of the Canaras about the beginnings of its population'. There is archeological proof that Neolithic man lived in Chicalim 70,000 years ago. In the eighth century Goan inhabitants were dark skinned, short statured and had simple life styles. The proto-astroloids followed these people—fishermen and boat builders who followed a lunar calendar. Then came the Dravidians, who were sophisticated city dwellers and had their own script. They practised yoga and a non-violent form of religion. The Aryans, a light-skinned, blue-eyed people, followed them. They brought a four-caste social system and spoke Sanskrit, a language rich in words and shades of meaning. Like all Indo-Europeans, the Aryans were adept at creating political systems.

The early settlers were intelligent and industrious. They soon organized themselves into well-administered villages with councils to arbitrate and manage community affairs. The land was fertile and well watered, with a pleasant climate, and the sea yielded a bounty of fish all year round. The people prospered and with prosperity came trade.

The beautiful port of Goa soon drew trade from overseas. Arab and Jewish vessels called, rich cargoes were unloaded from Indian ports and often from China and Malacca. Spices, gold, jewels, silks and grains exchanged hands. A city grew with the prosperity of the port—a city well planned, with sturdily built houses, roads and drains, and wells for water supply.

After accepting Hinduism, the lives of the people were governed in every possible way by the shastra or laws governing the Hindu way of life, and the daily routine of puja (prayer), work and leisure implanted a sense of stability and security. Interestingly, the people should have been vegetarians, but the Goan could not give up his favourite food—fish. The Bengali, Kashmiri and Goan Brahmins are the only non-vegetarian Brahmins in India.

During the third century AD, Goa came under the rule of various chiefs and overlords, some of whom called themselves kings. These were the Bhoja kings whose capital was present-day Chandor, the Chalukyas, the Silaharas, the Kadambas and finally the Yadavas of Devgiri. These were the Hindu dynasties, but they were rarely independent, coming under the suzerainty of powerful rulers on the other side of the ghats. However, for the common man, life was fairly peaceful. Herders and farmers, they followed the seasons of the year and paid taxes to whoever was in power. It is this philosophy of live and let live that makes the Goan a survivor.

Then, in the year 1294 AD came a Muslim invasion, so brutal that hardly a record remains of the time. The armies of Mohamed bin Tughlaq brought disorder, persecution and sheer terror, enough to throw an otherwise well-ordered society into utter confusion.

After this, Goa came under the suzerainty of successive Hindu rajas of Vijayanagar and Muslim sultans of the Bahamani dynasty. The land itself was spared direct involvement in the various wars between the two, and so for about 90 years, life carried on in comparative peace. The excellent natural harbour continued to attract trade and Goa gained wealth and fame.

In 1472, Goa again fell to the Bahamani armies and about ten years later, that kingdom was divided among three of its generals. Adil Shah, Sultan of Bijapur, claimed Goa.

Last of all, in 1520 came the Portuguese. They stayed for 450 years and gave to Goa that very special quality distilled from Iberian indolence, that distinct attitude of sossegado that sets Goans apart from other Indians.

These hard-bitten Iberians fell in love with the beauty of the land, its people, and of course, its wealth. Through it all, the Goans, though they fretted, plotted, and often rose in rebellion, had the wisdom to accept what they could not change. They adapted the strange ways of their conquerors to their own well-ordered customs, and in the process enriched and broadened their own culture.

One may assess a civilization by the extent to which its senses have developed in terms of art, literature, music and most importantly by the refinement of the food that is set on the table. Given the bounty of the land, Goans had long ago developed an appreciation for the finer things of life and an almost reverential attitude to food.

Careful preparation, subtle flavouring and elegant presentation of food is an art form in itself, and may take generations of dedicated and inspired cooks to evolve, a myriad influences directing and shaping that evolution. For Goa, most of that influence came from other countries. As a contemporary observer, Duarte Barbosa noted, 'It was a place of great trade, it has a good port to which flock many ships from Mekkah, Hormuiz, Cambay and the Malabar country. The town is very large with good edifices and handsome streets, surrounded by walls and towers. Some ships also come from China and Mallacca.'

Of course the Goan cooks eagerly experimented with all the spices and adopted some of the specialties and techniques of the many nationalities that trade brought to their shores. Contact with traders from far-away countries, conquering Muslim armies, and the availability of spices not native to the land, gave Goa's gourmets opportunities to widen and enrich their own repertoire of recipes. Perhaps the shewyo, made from steamed rice flour pressed through a sieve is a distant relative of Chinese noodles, and arroz refugado, made with rich meat stock and spicy Goa sausages, is the Goan version of the Mughlai biryani! Apparently, while soldiers and politicians played their games, the wise people of Goa quietly stole their recipes. However, they never lost sight of their native cuisine, and that is why Goa today sets a unique table. Food cooked in earthenware vessels on fires of coconut husk, twigs and wood has a very special flavour. The scent of wood seems to permeate the earthenware and works magic with its contents—spices, coconut milk and fish begin to 'belong' happily. Well water, feni and the love the cook adds, complete the formula!

The Bounty of the Land

Goa occupies a strip of land between the mountains of the Deccan and the Arabian Sea. The earth is a deep red, the sea blue-green, the sands as white as sugar and the tall coconut palms are green pom-poms against a clear blue sky. The higher reaches of the mountains are clad in thick forests, while the lower slopes are verdant with plantations of teak, cashew, mango, areca and bananas. Between the mountains and the beaches are the fields—lush through the year with successive crops of rice, vegetables and sugarcane. Between the fields and the breakers of the sea are the fabled beaches of Goa, reached through groves of coconut palms. These stretch for miles along the entire coastline, broken only by the occasional river mouth or rocky promontory.

The land itself undulates gently, rising to hills and sinking to level fields. It is a well-watered land with two major rivers—Zuari and Mandovi, and several smaller streams, as well as a network of canals making access to most areas fairly easy. The rivers at their mouths rise and fall with the tides. Along the lower reaches, thick mangroves protect the banks and the Khazan or reclaimed lands behind them from the wakes of passing boats, providing a rich breeding ground for small fish and the succulent Goa prawns.

The Khazan lands were reclaimed from the rivers many generations before the Portuguese arrived. Marshy areas were enclosed with bunds (dykes) built of tree trunks, stones and mud. Channels were dug to allow the water to run off during low tide and these had sluice gates to control the flow of water to the reclaimed fields. The bunds were meticulously inspected and repaired regularly. The reclaimed fields proved fertile, yielding bountiful harvests of the nutty flavoured red Goa rice, followed by vegetables—onions, dark red chillies, cabbages, kohlrabi, amaranthus, and the famous twelve-inch okras and fourteen-inch virvil beans, tender enough to eat raw. Every seven years, the tidal water is let in to flood the fields for several months to rid them of insect pests. When the water is let out, villagers harvest basketfuls of fat prawns and small fish galore. These are promptly and ruthlessly threaded onto sticks and roasted over a fire—sweet and succulent, they make a perfect accompaniment to a glass of feni.

There also existed in Goa a unique system of land sharing and cultivation. The first settlers, called Gauncars, set aside some of their fields to form a village trust or communidade to be tilled by the landless farmers. The farmers and donors shared the profit and the privilege passed on to the male descendants of the donors for generations. Even the Portuguese did not disturb the system, which continued until Goa was liberated in 1961.

History has yet to assess with fairness the part that Portugal played in Goa. No doubt they came in search of the fabulous riches of the East and to convert the natives to

Christianity—to 'civilize' them, and found a people already civilized, cultured, knowledgeable and skilled in every field of human activity.

However, among the Portuguese were men of vision and liberal ideas who could appreciate a well-ordered society wherever it was found. Fortune hunters aside, many of the Fidalgos, or nobles, were gentlemen farmers and horticulturists and the missionaries were certainly interested in building churches. These men struck a rapport with Goan landowners and farmers—men who took pride in coaxing the land to yield its best. They admired the skill of the Goan builders and artisans, the carvers of wood and stone, and with co-operation and encouragement persuaded them to build and decorate Goa's beautiful churches and monuments. They brought exotic trees, plants and fruit, sweet potato and tobacco, such as never had been seen before in Goa or in India from their colonies in Africa and Brazil.

'Portugal introduced chikoo, chilli, breadfruit, tobacco, pineapples, papaya, cashew, maize, mandicca, durian, sweet potato...', says J.B. Harrison. They also brought new species of mangoes. With careful nurturing in the rich soil, Goa soon produced a variety of mangoes, each unique in look, bouquet and flavour, ripening in succession so that from late April to late June the scent of mangoes fills the house. It would seem that the mango took to Goa—certainly, Goa took to the mango. Alfonso, malcurada, fernandino, xavier, monserrat—the connoisseur appreciated and relished each of them in turn and used them in pickles and preserves to be savoured for the rest of the year. Tender small mangoes are pickled in brine (chepnim); the larger raw ones are made into a pungent pickle (miscut) and the slightly ripe ones into chutneys. Some are dried in slivers and used in curry, some ripe ones are made into fruit leather, others cooked with sugar into a preserve (mangada), but the well ripened fruit are enjoyed by all. During the season, in ancestral homes, one storeroom is set aside for mangoes. These are lovingly stacked between layers of hay, and that storeroom is never locked. Small boys come along and eat until fit to burst. I know of one such home where the dining table sat forty adults, and mango eating contests were held after a full lunch, the prize going to the first to eat over twenty mangoes!

The cashew too throve in Goa and the clever Goan instead of discarding the cashew apple, presses the juice to make arrack and feni, while the nuts are roasted and sometimes dredged in spicy powders or in sugar—delectable dragees.

Rice is the staple grain, eaten as canji at eleven o'clock, and with curry—preferably fish curry—at lunch and dinner. Most of the sweets and desserts use rice as the main ingredient. There are quite a variety of rice grains, from the thick reddish round-grained nutty flavoured curmot to the fine-grained, highly polished suroi used in pulaus.

Nashni or ragi is next in importance, rich in minerals and vitamins, ground and roasted as bhakri (a thick chapatti). It is popular with labourers, because it is very sustaining.

As for the chilli, Goans soon developed a wide variety, from the huge dark red mild ones to the tiny, devil-red, button chillies that make the tongue curl. The type of chilli used makes all the difference to a dish. Thus a curry could be furious red in colour and yet be fairly mild in flavour, or look paler and be ferociously pungent.

The bounty of the seas and waters matched that of the land with no fewer than a hundred and seventeen varieties of fish being listed in the Goa gazetteer. Huge wiswond or surmai aptly called kingfish, rawas (salmon), shewto (mullet), baby shark, rayfish, mackerel, sardines, prawns of all sizes—the list is endless.

So, it is not surprising that Goans, all of them, from infants to senior citizens, from the labourers to the landlord, even the Saraswat Brahmin, consider a meal incomplete without fish in some form. To the Goan, fish is soul food and holds a special place in life. The famous Goan poet, Bakibab Borkar, addresses Yama, the god of death:

Please Sir, Mr God of Death
Don't make it my turn today
Not today
There is fish curry for dinner.

Fresh fish is a fetish with Goans. Indeed, not so long ago, when refrigeration first came to Goa, people would refuse to buy 'iced fish'. In the villages even today, fish provides an absorbing topic of conversation. 'I was in Mapuca bazaar and picked up some very fresh mussels, some tiger prawns . . . a handsome tsonkul . . . .' Small fish are strung in ganthons (garlands) and prawns are sold in vanté (small heaps). In Goa, it is the privilege of the man of the house to buy the fish. It is not sneaked home wrapped in paper, but carried proudly for all to see.

Goa is so fertile that every inch is either cultivated or overgrown! There is little grass and so grazing animals like cattle and goats are in short supply. However, it is rich pickings for foragers like chicken and pigs and every household kept a few chicken. The Portuguese taught converts how to eat pork, and pigs joined the backyard community. A chicken comes in handy to provide a meal for an unexpected guest, but meat of any sort is usually served on Sundays, feast days and celebrations.

In the days before freezers, all the meat had to be cooked or preserved as soon as an animal was slaughtered. The slaughter of a pig meant a busy week for the entire household. The meat was divided into suitable cuts for salt pork and sausages, while various curries took care of other cuts. Sorpotel, the famous pork and liver curry used the organs; vindaloo, the curry cooked without water, used the fattier pieces; aadmaas (bone curry), the bones and bouche, the tripe. What the family could not use was sold to the neighbours. Sausages alone took a whole week to make, and after that they had to be dried in the sun—small boys armed with sticks kept the inquisitive dogs at bay. The curries well doused in vinegar and feni had to be heated twice a day to keep them from spoiling, and by the end of a week were reduced to thick flavorsome sauces!

The jungles in the higher reaches of the ghats provided wild boar, venison and game, but only the jungle tribes enjoyed these meats.

While the Goan Hindu diet lays emphasis on vegetables, the Goan Christian merely tolerates vegetables and is content with a fresh salad of onions, cabbage and tomatoes. Most vegetables are cooked with a handful of tiny prawns—to make them palatable! While both Christian and Hindu diet featured fish prominently, the former inevitably took to the meat and sweet preparations of the Portuguese and so the Christian cuisine is far richer and more diverse.

Fortunately, some fruit is always in season in Goa—jackfruit, bullsheart, guava, melon, pineapple, chikoo and of course mango. Bananas are plentiful year round, from the small yellow ilchi to the huge, long red and yellow Moira bananas. Most houses had a clump of banana trees in the backyard.

With nature gifting such a vast cornucopia to Goa, is it any wonder that one Muslim invader declared that Goa was the closest thing to paradise on earth.

Seasons of the year

The seasons in Goa are best defined as wet, cool and dry, and hot and humid, the changes in temperature being marginal. However, the humidity is made bearable by the sea breezes. Goa's climate is typical of monsoon lands, a dry hot season increasing in humidity, followed by the monsoon rains which cool the air, then a dry cooler season which gradually gets hotter and more humid and the cycle is repeated. Temperatures in the villages are slightly cooler than in the cities, the thick tree cover providing some shade.

In late April and May, when the mercury soars, the fields are prepared for the all important rice crop. The previous year's stubble is burnt off, sods are turned and broken and cowdung and river mud spread as fertilizers. The sun blazes down mercilessly on the tillers who take an occasional break in a convenient copse of trees where water and canji refresh them. It is back breaking work indeed and the labourer certainly earns his copito (a half coconut shell) of urakh (the first distillate of feni, which is sweeter and milder) at the end of the day.

The first rains are eagerly awaited. The monsoon generally arrives by 12 June every year and if delayed causes great concern. People carry huge rocks on their heads in a penitential procession to the church, praying to St. Anthony for rain. Their prayers are invariably answered with apocalyptic storms. Thunder and lightning accompany the rain sheeting down. Only the brave venture out, as the village roads become watercourses. The family sits cosily in the balcão or porch, enjoying the pyrotechnics. The houses with their high roofs and overhanging eaves are cool and dry.

Goa storms are proverbial, but soon a pattern sets in. The fields turn emerald green with the young rice crop. The tillers in their bright clothes are strung out like luscious blooms, and their chanting voices carry on the breeze as they toil at weeding and transplanting the paddy. Fish becomes scarce as no boat dares venture out in the monsoon seas; besides it is the breeding season for fish. Vegetables begin to appear, and with a few dried prawns, tempt the appetite. The frugal housewife has a store of dried fish, pickles and powdered masalas as well as dried mango and jackfruit leather. The bamboo strung along the beam in the kitchen is heavy with onions hung within reach, and the feni is quietly maturing in the storeroom.

What more could one ask?

September brings a harvest not only of rice, but also of fish—mackerel, sardines, surmai, prawns and a dozen varieties of small fish, delicious in curries or just fried. The freshness of the fish revives the Goan heart. Farmers work frantically to get the grain in before the late showers that mark the end of the monsoon. The trees are clad in luxuriant foliage, birds sing their hearts out, replete with insects and ripening berries. Young women adorn their hair with strings of coral coloured abolim and white scented jasmine flowers, inspiring young swains to compose love songs. The themes are reminiscent of Portuguese fados or love songs—ill-fated love, unrequited love, doomed lovers—but the expressions are Goan. 'Angel of my bosom, my broken heart will never mend, I cry for you night and day . . . .' The harvest moon smiles benevolently down on all this foolishness and elders nod knowingly. Best of all, the sea has lost its fury and the beaches are safe again.

The newly harvested paddy is threshed, winnowed and dried in the sun. It is then parboiled in huge copper vessels, drained in large baskets and spread out to dry, first in the sun and then in the sala or main room of the house. The scent of paddy boiling over a wood fire is indescribably sweet and satisfying, reassuring one of the countless delicious meals to come. Paddy takes several days to dry thoroughly and has to be raked and stirred every day. At last it is filled into sacks and dispatched by bullock cart to be milled. Some of the inner red skin of the grain is left on. It is full of vitamins and imparts a distinctive flavour to the cooked rice. Brought home, it is filled into huge earthen jars and a few dried red chillies are added to keep away weevils.

Around this time of the year, fruit trees are cleared of monsoon parasites, and a manure of sea salt, river mud and rotting fish is spread among the roots—the secret of that special flavour in Goa mangoes?

The Goan Hindu marks the end of the monsoon with the observance of the Kartika full moon and Gokul Ashtami (Coconut day), as the sea begins to calm and fishing boats are re-launched.

With the advent of dry weather, the householder turns his attention to his dwelling. White ants are a constant menace, so beams and woodwork are inspected, repaired and painted with a preservative. The roof tiles may need relaying and the outside of the house has to be whitewashed. The annual whitewashing of the façade was a law in Portuguese times, but one that was easy to follow. The shells of clams and mussels consumed during the year were collected in an old oil drum, baked to form lime, and with the addition of water, some neel (a bluing agent) and some gum, made an excellent whitewash, free of cost!

In December, the cool season brings heavy morning dew. The fields are now a rich patchwork of onions, fat red Goa chillies, cabbages, tomatoes, okra and the well loved tambadi bhaji (red amaranthus). There seems to be no end to the procession of fish sellers hurrying along village roads, baskets laden with the silver of the sea.

The Christian housewife begins planning for Christmas. Coconuts are grated, ground, squeezed for milk and various sweets make an appearance—pastries like culculs, and neories; dodol, a type of dark halva;

bebinca, bol, and mandare (delectable papads made of rice and pumpkin, delicately tinted pink, green and yellow).

In February, the festival of Shigmo ushers in the spring, and then it is 'Carnaval' when Goa goes wild for a few days. Hordes of tourists flood into Goa for the festival, celebrated with dedicated Latin fervour. Since Liberation, there seems to be a distinct effort to emulate the Carnival of Rio de Janeiro, and the highlight is the parade of floats in the cities. The parade is led by the Lord of the Carnival, King Momo, whose proclamation of 'Fun and frolic shall reign for three days' is enthusiastically honoured, until Shrove Tuesday ushers in the sobriety of Lent. Fire and brimstone sermons in the churches have their effect and the evening copito of feni becomes a very necessary medicinal dose, but still gladdens the Goan heart! Soon May and the mango season starts the whole cycle again.

Cities may change and become bustling concrete mazes, but change comes slowly to the villages, the true heart of Goa. The leisurely cycle of the seasons, the evening visits to the taverna for the copito of feni, the gossip of the balcão, affirm that the pace of life in Goa remains sossegado—relaxed, unhurried, seductive, balm to the soul.

Goa is beautiful all year round, especially in the villages where life rolls on serenely, the momentum of millennia carrying it along.

Social interaction—the evolution of a mystique

The tides of history, which brought together two very different cultures for four hundred and fifty years, most

23

certainly left impressions on the people, the land and, specially for the purposes of this book, on the cuisine.

The Portuguese, enchanted by the beauty of the land, made Goa the capital of their Oriental Empire, calling it 'Perola do Oriente'—Pearl of the Orient, and 'Goâ Dourada'—Golden Goa. After they had converted a large part of the population to Christianity, they added ' Rome of the East'—certainly they built more churches than Rome ever had!

The majority of Goans were converted to Christianity and given the names of the priests who baptized them. It is common to find a whole village named 'Fernandes' or 'Rodrigues' or some equally Latin sounding name. Because Goan Christians bear Portuguese surnames, many outsiders classified them as mestizo (of mixed blood). In fact only a tiny minority are mestizo and Goans pride themselves on the purity of their descent, the caste system being one of the Hindu traditions they refuse to give up.

The Portuguese believed it to be their God-given mission to convert the Hindu 'natives' to Christianity, but met with stubborn opposition from most. Gentle persuasion gave way to blandishments and then coercion, often brutal. When offers of land, sinecures and advancement failed, the Portuguese resorted to legally justified measures. Laws were promulgated that forbade Hindu worship, temples were destroyed, and even the burning of corpses became a crime. One law punished anyone heard speaking a language other than Portuguese, another banned the use of salt in cooked rice, and a third decreed that converts prove their sincerity by eating pork and beef. Later they introduced the infamous Inquisition.

Many fled to the jungles around Ponda and to the areas beyond Portuguese rule, taking with them their ancient idols. Some fled to coastal and inland regions but they never forgot their gods in Goa. To this day, Goans of both Hindu and Christian descent make the pilgrimage to their family temples at Manguesh, Shanta Durga and Bandora.

Not all fled. Just opposite Old Goa, the two largest islands in the Mandovi River, Divar and Chorao, were inhabited by fiercely independent Hindu Brahmins who resisted all efforts to convert them. After all, the most important temple in Goa was on Divar, dedicated to the family deity of the Kadambas, that of Lord Shiva or Saptakoteshwar. The islanders patrolled the riverbanks day and night to repulse any invasion and even mounted night raids on the Portuguese garrison across the river. The Portuguese finally brought in crocodiles to deter the attacks. The descendants of these reptiles still live in the Mandovi and have become a tourist attraction.

It is said that the islanders were finally converted through trickery, but certainly a compromise was reached. The Hindu Brahmins agreed to conversion if allowed to retain their Hindu social customs. Finally the Pope himself, Gregory XV, passed a decree in 1623, which stated that Hindu converts would be allowed to keep their traditions 'such as the sacred thread and caste marks'. And so, paradoxically, Goan Christians remained Brahmin or Kshatriya and until recently, it was a rare and bold Goan Christian who married outside his caste!

With the advantages that conversion brought—land, education, employment and advancement—Christians became the dominant community, owning vast properties, building gracious mansions, adopting a lifestyle in imitation of the Portuguese in language, manners and dress. While it may have been profitable to speak, read and write Portuguese, the language of the traditional Goan remained Konkani, which can be elaborately polite or disdainfully contemptuous, heartbreakingly amorous or devastatingly pungent. Inevitably, the stage and plays became the perfect vehicle for people to comment on life with the Portuguese with allusions and nuances of meaning that only the locals fully appreciated and understood.

Konkani tiatra or theatre flourishes even today, every performance eagerly awaited, and packed. A unique form of entertainment, the main play has a serious theme—often with a moral—interspersed with comic relief. The clowns provide comments and songs on topical news and events, the political scene being a favourite target for the clever, sharp barbs of the script.

Meanwhile, Portugal as an empire declined in importance and Goa was just a very distant outpost of a once powerful nation. Portugal, itself sinking to become one of the least developed European countries, did little to develop Goa's rich natural resources. Proposals in the early twentieth century to harness the Dudhsagar falls for power were turned down, while a project to develop the sugarcane industry was almost ridiculed: 'Imported sugar is much cheaper'. Incredibly, barring fresh fish, rice, mangoes and vegetables, all other articles of food, textiles, toiletries and even some building materials were imported from overseas or over the border. In fact, it was the Japanese who mined manganese ore in the fifties, shipping out entire hillsides with their dedicated efficiency. The aspirations of a people were ignored by a colonial power in decline.

With only village industries active, opportunities for employment were meagre. Education in Portuguese offered only two disciplines at the college level, law and medicine, the latter being merely a licentiate. With neither scope nor prospects for their talents, many Goans, especially the Christians, emigrated to other parts of India and to every continent in the world. The world may not have known Goa, but Goans knew the world. They achieved recognition and fame in the arts and sciences, in law and administration, but never forgot their roots in Goa. The immigrant might conform in dress and language, but he never quite gave up his eating style. He could not have survived without his fish curry and rice—it was an assertion of his identity!

The people of Goa are outgoing, warm-hearted and passionate, with a zest for life. They are fond of music, dancing and good food, very proud of their beautiful land and with a deep sense of their own importance in the scheme of things. Every Goan owns his own dwelling in the village of his origin, be it ever so humble. The wealthy built vast mansions with ballrooms and chandeliers, some even had a coat of arms, but most people built spacious comfortable bungalows. Interestingly, despite their Western outward look, the houses were laid out according to the traditional Hindu Vaastu Shastra—the ancient building guidelines. One room, the sala, was set aside for receiving visitors while the family enjoyed its privacy in the rest of the house. An inner courtyard or angan preserved the Hindu tradition of family seclusion. The houses with their balcãos, wide verandas and well-kept gardens made up a settlement not unlike a European village. Parts of Old Panjim could have been in Lisbon and the waterfront with its pillared balustrade could have belonged to the Riviera. The tree-shaded squares and roads and the general air of somnolence was Iberian.

The Goan is a Goan first and a Hindu or Christian afterwards. His roots go back to a civilization that was common to both and which retained an identity despite the many cultures with which it interacted. The two communities live together peacefully, respecting the other's right to his particular form of worship. Indeed, so strong and deep are the roots that Christian Goans still believe in the evil eye or dheeshth, and in a somewhat bizarre ritual, salt and red chillies are passed over the sufferer while reciting Christian prayers. Not even the parish priest finds it odd! Christians and Hindus freely attend each other's services and festivals.

A Hindu Brahmin has acquired my great-grandfather's house in Divar. He has not disturbed the little oratory in the wall with its crucifix and statues of saints—indeed, he keeps the lamp burning there night and day. In the next room, a lamp also burns before his family gods and he is meticulous about his daily puja.

I wonder if such a situation could obtain anywhere else in India.

Celebrations and Festivals

Goa loves a celebration, and barring the monsoons, every

month brings a saint's day or festival to celebrate. Besides these, people often organize a novena at one of the many wayside chapels or crosses, ending with a ladorinha or litany sung to the accompaniment of a squeaky violin. The evening concludes with the mandatory round of boiled gram and feni.

A church or temple feast means sweets. Stalls are set up selling confections special to feast days—sugared cashew nuts, nutty ginger and jaggery squares, twig-like kadio-bodio made with gram flour, and ladoos of all kinds, some as big as cannon balls. Of course, in a corner, hidden behind a massive tree, the owner of the local taverna sells feni and beer to revive those worn out by sermon and ceremony. What can be most unnerving are the firecrackers set off at the most solemn moment of the service by gleeful young boys, their special delight being a cracker called the gornal or thunder. The explosion echoes in the surrounding hills and sets the village dogs yelping in terror.

An interesting festival marks the start of the harvest season. Before the Portuguese came, the bhatt or high priest would lead a procession to the fields and cut the first sheaf. This was carried amidst joyful song and dance to the temple and offered to the gods. A very special sweet is made at this time called pathoyeo. Rice is soaked, ground and spread over the leaves of the turmeric plant, which is in season at this time. Scraped coconut and palm jaggery is mixed and spread over the rice, the leaf is folded, sealed and steamed. The rice pastry takes on the flavour of the leaves—indeed, the house is redolent with the fragrance. With the advent of Christianity, the Goans substituted the parish priest for the bhatt and the church for the temple, but the pathoyeo still remains.

Other Hindu festivals like Shigmo, the spring festival, Nautara or nine nights in September, the feast of Hanuman and Coconut day when boats are launched after the monsoons, are observed throughout Goa. The spring festival of Shigmo is very much a village festival, especially in what used to be the border villages of the original Portuguese territory. These villages were often raided by the Ranés, a tribe living in the nearby areas, sworn enemies of the Portuguese. Their swift and ruthless looting made them feared and dreaded and in the area around Aldona, houses were built with rifle slits and secret hiding places for the women and children. These raids are re-enacted at Shigmo. Dancers wear horse costumes—a cane framework with a horse's neck and head, tied to the waist and draped over with the wearer's long garment. The beat of the drums echoes the gallop of the horses as the procession thunders and whirls through the village. Five days of festivity follow, marked by the staging of historical and morality plays, ending with Holi and the sprinkling of coloured powders and water on the participants.

The Christians observe the feasts of the church calendar, but the greatest celebration is reserved for the village church or chapel on the feast days of their patron saints. The church or chapel is decorated with paper flags and lanterns; arches of palm fronds mark the route of the procession; silken banners hang above the altar; and above the aisle, paper flowers and angels spill out of hanging baskets. The various confrairias or associations of church helpers, wearing the capes and medallions of their fraternity, carry tall candles in procession around the church compound.

In some villages the privilege of celebrating the feast—arranging and paying for preacher, music, decorations and fireworks—was confined to the families of the gauncars who did the honour in turns. Today, with costs escalating, two or three families jointly bear the expenses. The chief patron of the feast gives a lavish lunch for about fifty special guests, complete with speeches and toasts. A whole roast suckling pig is 'a must', with fish and chicken in various guises, and of course, at least three desserts. Needless to say, beer, whisky and feni flow like water—after all, the honour of the village and that of the host are at stake.

A village wedding is the best of all celebrations. It allows the Goan free rein to his many talents—arranging for the music, helping with the decorations and especially being involved with the food and drink of the banquet—puts a sparkle in his eye and a spring to his step. A son or daughter of the village belongs to every one of its families. It is the warm genuine affection of people who knew one's parents and grandparents, that makes a wedding day memorable.

In towns, a hall can be hired and a caterer arranged, a rather impersonal affair. It is the traditional wedding in the village that reveals the true Goan, Hindu or Christian. As with special events the world over, Goa village weddings too have adjusted to the demands of modern life, but the old order remained until Liberation.

A Hindu wedding ceremony was much the same as in the rest of India, celebrated according to Vedic rites. On the auspicious day, a pit for the sacred fire was dug under a pandal. The village bhatt conducted the ceremony. Gifts were exchanged and the families congratulated each other. After that, the festivities continued for a few days, depending on the social status of the families. Under a brightly coloured pandal relays of guests were welcomed and fed. They dined seated on white cloth spread on the ground, and ate off banana leaves. The food was likely to be vegetarian, sometimes a chicken or mutton xacuti or curry might be served in a secluded room for the men. A sweet, a ladoo or a modak shaped like a flower bud, provided a foil for the rich curries and pickles eaten with rice and ghee. Special sweets and fruit were served for dessert. Liquor was rarely, and ever so discreetly, served.

The Hindu gentleman's dress was fairly simple: the dhoti was spotless white, fine-spun cotton or pure silk with coloured or gold borders. The Hindu matron was regal in her traditional nine-yard sari worn kasotho style (drawn between the legs with the pleats trailing behind like a short train). Her jewellery was traditional too, gold hair ornaments, heavy jewelled nose ring, ear rings, bangles, and necklaces of gold set with precious stones, including the mangal-sutra or wedding necklace, and heavy silver anklets on her feet. Fresh, sweet-scented jasmine, champak and keora in her hair completed the toilette. The bride wore a sari of red and green with heavy jewellery. She sat demurely with her face veiled in jasmine flowers.

Goan Christian weddings evolved into elaborate affairs, borrowing toasts, speeches and ballroom dancing from the Portuguese while retaining several Hindu customs. For instance, a few days before the wedding, huge trays laden with special sweets—dodol, doce baji and bolinhas, and fruit—bananas being mandatory—were dispatched to the bridegroom's house to be distributed in his neighbourhood. This was called ojem and was an invitation to the wedding to those who received it. The engagement ring on a small tray with the image of the infant Jesus accompanied the ojem and was duly admired and blessed.

Another favourite wedding rite practiced by both Hindus and Christians is the rhos or the bathing of the bride in coconut milk and turmeric, followed by the wearing of green, red and yellow bangles. A few days before the wedding, women relatives gather at the bride's house. They grind about fifteen coconuts with just enough turmeric to give the bride's skin a golden glow and then squeeze out the milk. They sit around the bride and sing couplets in praise of her beauty and talents, and to bless her marriage, while they take turns to pour a measure of rhos over her. After she has bathed and changed, the bangle seller arrives. Now the women buy green, red and yellow glass bangles and as they slip them over her hands, they sing praises and blessings. Tears and laughter mingle with the songs which say 'Your parents are so sad . . . you are leaving your childhood home . . . you will take the light of your beauty to your husband's home . . . may you be blessed with many children . . . do not forget us . . .' and more in the same vein.

Weeks before the wedding, sugar, flour, rice, ghee, jaggery and coconuts are bought and stored. Eggs, chicken and fish are arranged for, and hapless piglets and porkers are booked for the feast. One storeroom is set aside for the liquor—cashew and palm feni, wines, beer and whisky, the beverages—orchata, the almond syrup and syrups of brindão or kokum and lime, crockery, glassware and cutlery, most of the latter borrowed from willing neighbours.

Three or four days before the wedding, a makeshift kitchen is set up in the compound of the house. The professional cooks arrive with their equipment; huge copper kyles or pans used for frying—some flat and some as deep as a wok—and the shallow clay kundlem or the cooking pots. The cooks range in expertise from temperamental chefs of haute cuisine to women cooks who work wonders with ordinary spices and ingredients.

They start with the pork dishes—sorpotel, cabidela and vindaloo, for they must mature in the huge clay vessels, heated through every day to preserve them. Then the desserts are prepared—many-layered bebinca, leitria with a filigree of yellow crowning the tender coconut in sugar, darkest brown dodol made of jaggery, coconut and rice, marzipan dedos de dama dipped in caramel, cobwebs of tender coconut on dainty paper doilies, etc. The day before the wedding it is the turn of the chicken and suckling pigs to be curried and roasted. Last of all, seafood dishes are readied—prawns in various guises, oysters, surmai stuffed and grilled, and the highly prized rawas perhaps cooked Portuguese style. A vast cauldron of sopa grossa is 'a must', rich with slivers of chicken, olives and olive oil. The cooks work through the night and tantalizing odours waft through the village. It is amazing how, with only basic equipment, a banquet fit for a king is readied for the table.

Meanwhile, on the other side of the house, a pandal is

erected. Bright coloured awnings are stretched on a bamboo framework to provide shade, the floor is swept and thoroughly doused to settle the dust, chairs and tables are set out, and the whole area is decorated with palm fronds, paper flags and lanterns, and fresh flowers.

The church too is decorated and on the great day, the guests begin to arrive in their finery. In imitation of the Portuguese, the upper-class women wore gowns and frocks, with jewellery in the Oporto style, or perhaps a dainty version of the foddo. The men wore dark suits. Indeed, before Liberation, the bridegroom proudly strutted around in a morning coat, striped trousers, top hat and gloves.

However, it was the sari-clad Christian woman who proudly wore traditional Goan jewellery, much of it heirloom. Besides the jet and gold rosary fifteen decades old, three necklaces and triple ear-tops were the minimum in pre-Liberation Goa. First a choker, a gold mesh ribbon set with a jewelled dove called the fugdo, then the foddo or fator, three oblongs of malachite bound in filigree gold, joined by thick double strands of gold chain and last of all the cordao, a heavy, linked gold chain reaching to the waist. Other gold collars and necklaces set with coral roses, diamonds or gold dust stones could be added, according to the wearer's status and wealth. Her ears, pierced at three points, received carabs, delicate gold studs set with malachite and joined by fine gold chains. She wore several rings, bracelets and bangles of gold and her hair was dressed with gold pins and fresh flowers. Goa goldsmiths to this day enjoy a high reputation for fine workmanship.

The bride wore a rich sari of white and gold silk, white being the western Christian tradition, and with it a set of heavy gold jewellery gifted by the bridegroom. Her blouse was always high necked and long sleeved, her hair was elaborately dressed with gold pins and fresh flowers. Footwear called chinelam, mules of gold embroidered velvet in red or royal blue, were worn by all women.

A wedding in a Salcete village could bring forth a thoddup bazu clad woman. The thoddup was a kind of lungi reminiscent of Malaysia, worn on special occasions with a richly embroidered panel down the front, and the bazu was a high-necked, long-sleeved jacket. It was worn with a delicate stole of lace.

Interestingly, until the mid-fifties, all matrons attending church services wore the ohl over the sari or thoddup bazu. This consisted of two lengths of white cotton or silk, one worn like a lungi, the other worn over the head with the finely pleated ends tucked into the waist at the back—a truly unique attire. Today, much less jewellery is worn, and the bride may wear a Western style gown, more is the pity.

The village band is an important element of feasts and weddings, providing pomp and circumstance to the occasion. At a wedding, it escorts the bride to church, returning after the ceremony with the entire congregation. It is welcomed with a barrage of firecrackers and makes a ceremonial round of the pandal. The cake is cut, toasts are raised, and the dancing, led by the bridal couple, starts in the sala of the house.

The highlight is the bridal mando. This is danced to a song, which is often specially composed for the bridal couple. Iberian influence is clear in the slow, dirge-like cadences, but the irrepressible Goan spirit takes over with the dulpads or couplets. The Pavanne like steps give way to a quickened beat and the dancers whirl and stamp, the women's eyes flash provocatively over their fans and the men's kerchiefs flick the air with every turn. The lines of men and women advance and retreat, cross and re-cross, closer and closer, but they never touch. The dance ends in a lively progress in and out and around the house until a point of near collapse is reached. In content and tempo, the mando is pure Goan with just a touch of the Portuguese to make it a unique blend of Indian and Iberian.

Now it is time for the wedding feast, and the veritable banquet laid out has not changed much over the years. Tables groan with food. Whole roast stuffed piglings, stuffed, baked fish, oyster pie, prawn pie, curried and fried prawns and fish, chicken in aspic, chicken xacuti, sorpotel, pulaus, oddé (puris), sana (steamed rice cakes)—every inch of the table is covered. Desserts are laid out along the middle—bebinca, leitria, crème de caramel, dedos de dama—a bewildering array. The band plays soft music and the talk subsides as guests demolish seemingly endless replenishments. Small boys eat until they are ready to burst. The host and hostess urge the guests to 'have a little bit more' till all are replete. A benevolent somnolence descends on all. Good food, plenty of liquor and sentimental music work their magic and guests begin to leave before they succumb.

However, the celebrations are not over till the tornaboda or return feast. This is one last celebration, which is de rigueur, a banquet almost as elaborate as the wedding feast itself. It is hosted by 'the other side' and mercifully held a few days later.

The Goan can make an occasion of any event, and even a funeral is conducted with great pomp and solemnity. The Goan Hindu funeral has always been fairly austere. After prayers in the house, the body is carried to the burning ghats escorted by the male relatives. The eldest son carries a pot of live coals. He calls out thrice to his father to make sure he is dead, then lights the pyre. No food is cooked in the house until the purification rites are held.

It is a far more elaborate affair with the Goan Christian funeral, where the Iberian influence is marked. Men and women arrive clad in black—not so long ago a full black suit was mandatory for men, regardless of the temperature. There is much wailing—in fact, certain women in the village had a reputation as professional mourners, and were often asked to attend.

The village band wearing black armbands escorted the hearse to the church playing Mozart's *Funeral March* with ghoulish relish. At the graveside, a friend or relative would deliver an oration in an extravagant and flowery style and the professional mourners would raise a wail as the coffin was lowered into the grave.

In the bereaved household, food and drink had to be readied for those coming from afar. Indeed, some would have to spend the night, sleeping on mats in the sala. Fortunately, neighbours brought cooked food and bedding to help out.

Both history and legend agree that the first settlers in Goa were men of peace. Cowherds they might have been, but something in them responded to the beauty and tranquillity of the sandbank. Perhaps they felt a gentler way of life was possible here. Certainly they were well content, their settlements flourished, and the people themselves could develop the quality that today marks the Goan identity—a calm self-confidence that accepts whatever life has to offer and makes the best of it. For the Goan, life is to be savoured, to be enjoyed; and so he becomes an epicure and a gourmet, developing a taste for good food, good liquor, good music, and good friends to share it all.

Keeping a good table is a matter of honour with the Goan. Whether the food is simple or elaborate, care and patience is taken over the preparation. Goan food simply cannot be hurried. As Owen Meredith wrote:

We may live without poetry, music and art
We may live without conscience and live without heart
We may live without friends;
We may live without books
But civilized man cannot live without cooks.

GOAN CUISINE

Almost every Goan recipe requires slow cooking, on low to medium heat. This gives the flavours time to meld.

The dried red chillies used are the Kashmiri chillies, which are long, curly and crinkly looking, unless otherwise stated.

Fish and meat is always cleaned, cut, rinsed and lightly salted before cooking. Most meat recipes call for a marinating time before cooking.

Rice:
Three varieties of rice were traditionally grown in Goa.

The thickest was the curmot—round grained and very sustaining. It was thus favoured by the labourers. It is so delicious, it can be eaten plain.

The mundo is a slightly slimmer grained rice and was most popular. It was eaten with the daily fish curry and was used in almost every dish, sweet or savoury.

These two varieties were parboiled then milled, but some of the red coating was left on the grain, imparting a unique colour and nutty flavour to the cooked rice.

The finest grained rice is the suroi, used in pulaus. This variety was not parboiled, but milled to remove all the red coating on the grain.

To Cook Goa Rice:
Goa rice is usually soaked for about 15 minutes before cooking.

If using a pressure cooker, add 2½ cups water to one cup rice. Add salt to taste at the start of cooking. After the cooker has reached its pressure—first whistle, lower heat and cook for about 10 minutes more. Allow the cooker to cool on its own before opening.

If cooking rice in a pan, use 3½ cups water to one cup rice. Bring water to the boil, add the soaked rice and bring to boil again. Lower heat and allow to simmer for about 20 minutes till done. To test if ready, press a few grains between your fingers. There should be no hard kernel left. Add salt just before rice is done. Drain and keep warm.

Coconuts:
Goan recipes call for at least three different types of coconuts.

- Fully ripe coconut: It is covered with a dry brown fibrous husk and has a thick firm flesh. This is used in all curries. It is either ground to a paste with other spices or the extracted milk is used. The extracted milk is also used in sweet preparations. The grated coconut is used for vegetables.

- Semi-ripe coconut: It is green-brown on the outside, with a whitish husk covering the shell. The flesh when chewed does not leave a residue in the mouth, as does the fully ripe coconut. These are used in sweets like letria, coconut pies, etc., where grated or ground coconut is required.

- The tender coconut: This is the third variety which has flesh about ⅛" thick. It is tender, but firm enough to cut into strips and is used for dishes like Teias de Aranha or Cobwebs.

Very tender coconuts are not used for cooking. The husk is green and they have hardly any flesh but they provide us with delicious, sweet coconut water.

To extract coconut milk:
One coconut should yield about 250 gms of grated coconut. Place the grated coconut in a grinder with half a cup of warm water. Grind for about 30 seconds. The mixture should be reduced to a cohesive mass.

Place a strainer lined with muslin over a pan and squeeze ground coconut by the handful over the strainer. This will give you about one cup of thick coconut milk. It is always added towards the end of the cooking process.

Add 2½ cups hot water to the residue coconut. Stir to mix and allow to cool. Squeeze out the milk in another pan over a muslin-lined strainer. You should get 2 cups milk. This is the thin coconut milk and may be added at an earlier stage of the cooking process.

Souring agents:
Goan cuisine uses a number of souring agents. These are usually added towards the end of the cooking process.

- Vinegar is not normally used in vegetable dishes, except when cooking okra, where it helps remove stickiness. Its main use is in meat and fish preparations.

- Sliced raw mango is used during the season along with other souring agents for additional tartness.

- Kokum or brindão is a variety of dried Indian sour plum. It is normally used while cooking deep sea fish like mackerel, sting ray, baby shark etc. It is sometimes added to vegetables.

- Biblim is a cucumber-like vegetable that hangs in bunches on the trunk of the tree. It is also known as morello cherry and mainly used in fish curries.

- Tefla are lemon flavoured berries usually used dry for deep sea fish preparations.

- Tamarind is the most commonly used souring agent in Goan cuisine. The extracted pulp is used for vegetable, meat and fish preparations.

To extract tamarind pulp:
Soak a walnut sized ball of tamarind in ½ cup hot water for 10 minutes. Loosen and work the tamarind with your fingers, till the pulp leaves the pith. Squeeze pulp over a strainer into a pan.

Toddy and feni:
Toddy and feni are frequently used in Goan cuisine to give the dish that extra zing.

Substitute for toddy:

- Fresh coconut water from the very tender coconut, kept in a warm place for 1-2 days.

- One tablespoon of feni plus four teaspoons baking powder, dissolved in 1 cup water.

Substitute for feni:
There is no real substitute for feni, but Tequila may be used, failing which, vodka or white wine will do.

TABLE OF MEASURES

The cup measure used in this book is an 8 oz cup (225 ml)

1 tsp = 5 ml
1 tbsp = 3 tsp
2 tbsp = 30 gm
A pinch = 1/8 tsp (literally a pinch)
A dash = 1-2 drops

All spoon measures are level

Metric Equivalent					
Metric Unit	Oz/ fl.oz	American Pint	American Cup	Imperial Pint	Imperial Cup
30	1				
60	2				
85	3				
115	4	¼	½		
140	5			¼	½
170	6				
200	7				
225	8	½	1		
255	9				
285	10			½	1
310	11				
340	12	¾			
370	13				
395	14				
425	15		¾		
455	16	1			
480	17				
510	18				
540	19				
570	20			1	
1kg	2.2				
1 litre			2		1¾

OVEN TEMPERATURES			
Description	Celsius (°C)	Fahrenheit (°F)	Gas Mark
Cool	110	225	¼
	120	250	½
Very slow	135	275	1
	150	300	2
Slow	160	325	3
Moderate	175	350	4
	190	375	5
Moderately hot	200	400	6
Fairly hot	220	425	7
Hot	230	450	8
Very hot	245	475	9
Extremely hot	260	500	10

BASIC MASALA

RECHEIO MASALA

Makes: 1 cup

A great stand-by for the busy housewife, this combination of spices goes well with fish, fowl and flesh, and every Goan household keeps a supply handy. Maria Felicia had this masala ground by the kilo. The maid/cook would have to rub oil into her hands to lessen the sting of the chillies. Usually, a 'rogdo' was used, a massive semi-sphere of stone with a hollow in the centre into which fitted a club-like 'pestle'. This was rotated with the right hand while the left hand kept pushing the masalas back into the hollow. It needed some skill to prevent one's fingers from becoming part of the masala!

20 dried red Kashmiri chillies
3 large cloves
1 pod garlic
1 tsp cumin seeds
8 peppercorns
4" piece cinnamon
2 tsp turmeric powder
Seeds of 6 green cardamoms
Pulp from tamarind the size of a small walnut soaked in ½ cup
water Vinegar to grind

- Grind all ingredients in vinegar to a smooth paste and store in an airtight jar.

BAFAD MASALA

Makes: 1½ cups

Another stand-by, especially for beef and mutton dishes. The Goan precursor to the 'East Indian' bottle masala and the closest any Goan cook will come to 'curry powder'!

½ kg dried red Kashmiri chillies
25 gm cinnamon
25 gm peppercorns
25 gm turmeric powder
2 cups coriander seeds
25 gm cloves
1½ tbsp cumin seeds

- Grind all spices to a powder.

- Store in an airtight jar.

- Use in the proportion of one tablespoon to ¾ kg of meat.

SAMBAR MASALA

Makes: 2 cups

This masala is normally made for use during the monsoon months. It is particularly good with Bengal gram.

2 tbsp cumin seeds
4 tbsp coriander seeds
1 tbsp mustard seeds

½ tbsp dill (sua) seeds
½ tbsp cloves
1 tbsp peppercorn
4" piece cinnamon
3" piece whole turmeric
25 dried red chillies
1 tbsp rice

- Roast each ingredient except rice separately on a tava or griddle over medium to low heat. Stir continuously while roasting and take care not to brown spices. Remove from heat when aroma of spice arises. Cool.

- Mix all spices except chillies with rice.

- Grind to a fine powder.

- Grind chillies to a fine powder.

- Mix well together.

- Store in an airtight jar.

Appetizers

Entertaining in Goa is a leisurely affair and dinner is rarely announced before 10 p.m. While the host feels that it is his duty to ensure that his guests never hold an empty glass, the hostess provides a steady stream of delicious titbits, a foretaste of what awaits at the table. The variety and daintiness of the snacks enhances the culinary reputation of the hostess.

FOFOS
Fish Rolls

Makes: 24 rolls

The classic fofos of Portugal were made with bacalhau or salt cod, alas, not available in India. Goan cooks adapted the recipe to fish or prawns.

1 cup cooked flaked fish or chopped raw prawns, deveined and cleaned
1 egg, white and yolk separated
1 onion, finely chopped
1 medium potato, boiled and mashed
2 cloves garlic, ground
1 green chilli, deseeded and finely chopped
2 tbsp cornflour
Fish stock to moisten
Salt and pepper
Oil for deep frying

- Beat egg white till stiff.

- Combine remaining ingredients except oil. Form into small rolls.

- Heat oil in a deep frying pan. Dip fofos in egg white and deep fry till golden. Drain on paper towel.

- Serve hot.

- A tomato-chilli sauce makes a good dip.

TORRADAS DE CAMARÃO
Prawn Toasts

Makes: 20 toasts

The toasts are best eaten freshly fried, before they become soggy and tough—but make plenty, they prove hard to resist.

1 cup small shelled prawns, cleaned and deveined
1 tbsp oil
2 large onions, finely chopped
½" piece ginger, finely chopped
2 cloves garlic, finely chopped
3 green chillies, deseeded and finely chopped
1 large tomato, chopped
½ tsp powdered cloves
1 tbsp chopped fresh coriander leaves
Salt to taste
¼ cup fresh breadcrumbs
5 slices stale bread, crust removed and cut into quarters
1 large egg beaten with a little milk
Oil for deep frying
Strips of tomato or capsicum for garnish

- Chop prawns if large and lightly salt.

- Heat one tablespoon oil in a pan and fry onions over medium heat till pale gold in colour.

- Add ginger, garlic and chillies, and cook for one minute. Add tomato and cook till soft.

- Stir in prawns and cook only till they turn pink and curl up. Overcooking makes prawns tough.

- Remove from heat, sprinkle over cloves and coriander leaves.

- Adjust seasoning.

- Stir in just enough breadcrumbs to keep mixture moist but not dry.

- Place a small quantity of mixture on each bread square, pressing it on.

- Heat oil for frying in a deep frying pan. Dip toasts in beaten egg and deep fry till golden brown.

- Drain on paper towel and serve hot, garnished with strips of tomato or capsicum.

RISSÓIS DE CAMARÃO
Prawn turnovers

Makes: 24-30 rissóis

Dainty little turnovers, which are served as appetizers—make plenty, as they disappear fast. This is Tatiana's recipe and she stores them in the deep freezer to be fried when needed. They keep for a week.

Pastry:

2 cups refined flour (maida)
2 cups water
½ tsp salt
1 tbsp butter

Filling:

¾ cup shelled prawns, cleaned and deveined
2 tbsp oil
1 cup finely chopped onion
2 green chillies, deseeded and chopped
2 cloves garlic, finely sliced
½ cup water
Salt and pepper to taste
1 tbsp cornflour
1 tbsp grated cheese

Oil for deep frying
1 egg, beaten
Breadcrumbs for coating

Pastry:

• Sieve flour.

- Place water in a pan with salt and bring to boil. Add butter, lower heat and add flour. Stir and beat to mix till it forms a ball.

- Remove from heat and allow to cool—enough to handle. Knead well.

Filling:

- Chop prawns if large.

- Heat 2 tablespoons oil in a pan and fry onions, chillies and garlic till onions are transparent.

- Add prawn and cook till they turn light pink. Stir in water, salt and pepper and cook for 2 minutes.

- Mix cornflour with a little water and stir into mixture. Cook till thick and creamy. Remove from heat and add cheese. Mix well and allow to cool.

To *prepare rissóis*:

- Roll out pastry about ⅛" thick. Cut out rounds about 2" in diameter.

- Place one teaspoon filling on each round, fold over and moisten to seal.

- Heat oil in a deep frying pan. Dip rissóis in beaten egg, roll in breadcrumbs and deep fry.

- Drain on paper towel and serve hot.

ALMONDEGAS DE CAMARÃO
Prawn Cakes

Makes: 12-14 cakes

These are utterly delectable. Made in a larger size they can serve as a main dish, but the bite-size cakes make excellent cocktail snacks. My Uncle Fred still waters at the mouth forty year later when he recalls my Grandmother's almodegas!

1 cup shelled prawns, cleaned, deveined and lightly salted (save tails for garnish)
½ coconut, grated
4 green chillies, deseeded if desired
½" piece fresh ginger
6 cloves garlic
1 small onion, chopped
1 tsp cumin powder
½ tsp turmeric powder
½ cup fresh breadcrumbs
1 egg, beaten
Salt to taste
Oil for shallow frying

Finely ground:

4 cloves
1" piece cinnamon
8 peppercorns

Garnish:

Prawn tails
Sprigs of coriander leaves

C

- Cook prawns in one tablespoon water over low heat, stirring to avoid sticking. Cool.

- Grind prawns, coconut, chillies, ginger, garlic and onion coarsely. Mix in powdered and ground spices and breadcrumbs. Add enough beaten egg to bind. Add salt to taste and mix well.

- Oil hands and take up large walnut sized portions of mixture. Shape into flat cakes. Stick a prawn tail into each cake to give a festive presentation.

- Heat oil in a pan and shallow fry cakes.

- Serve hot, garnished with sprigs of fresh coriander leaves.

PAPARIS RECHEADOS
Stuffed Papads

Makes: 24

Use small papads made of urad dal (black beans). When cut in half and folded over, they make a dainty snack. Since papads cook fast, the oil must not be too hot or they will burn and taste bitter.

12 fresh and pliant papads
A little flour and water to make a paste for sealing papads
Oil for deep frying

Filling:
1 cup shelled prawns, cleaned, deveined and lightly salted
1 tbsp oil
3 medium onions, chopped
4 cloves garlic, finely chopped
¼" piece ginger, finely chopped
4 green chillies, finely chopped
3 medium potatoes, boiled and cut into small cubes
Salt to taste
1 tbsp fresh coriander leaves, chopped
3 cloves, powdered

- Chop prawns if large.

- Heat one tablespoon oil in a pan and fry onions till opaque. Add garlic, ginger and green chillies.

- Stir in potatoes and cook for one minute. Add prawns and mix well. Cook only till prawns curl up. Add salt to taste. Sprinkle over coriander leaves and clove powder.

- Mix well and allow to cool.

- Make a thick paste with a little flour and water. Cut each papad in half, place a little mixture on one side, fold over papad and seal with flour paste.

- Heat oil in a deep frying pan and deep fry papad parcels. Drain on paper towel and serve hot with green chutney or tomato sauce.

Note: If the papads are not pliant, pass them under running water.

PASTEIS DE OSTRAS
Oyster Patties

Makes: 20-24 patties

It is almost impossible to produce puff pastry in a tropical climate, and more so with primitive cooking facilities, so innovative cooks devised this fried version. The secret lies in patient frying of the patties, but the results are worth the effort. It has to be a very special occasion that calls for oyster patties, among the most elegant of appetizers.

Dough:

¾ kg (6 cups) refined flour (maida)
½ tsp salt
4-5 tbsp ghee (clarified butter) or vanaspati
3 tbsp fine rice flour

Filling:

1 tbsp olive oil
2 medium onions, finely chopped
½" piece ginger, finely minced
6 cloves garlic, finely minced
4 green chillies, deseeded and minced
Salt to taste
2-3 tbsp white wine
½ kg oysters, cleaned and shelled

Oil or vanaspati for deep frying

Garnish:

Sprigs of parsley, celery and fresh coriander

Dough:

- Mix flour and salt with enough water to make a firm dough.

- Mix vanaspati or ghee and rice flour to spreading consistency.

- Roll out dough about ⅛" thick, spread with rice flour mixture and fold as for puff pastry—fold in 3, then fold length in 3. Roll out again and spread with rice flour mixture.

- Fold and roll out again. Repeat till all the mixture has been used.

- Let dough rest in a cool place.

Filling:

- Heat olive oil in a pan and fry onions till opaque. Add ginger, garlic and chillies and fry, mashing mixture with back of spoon till it forms a thick sauce. Add salt.

- Lower heat and add wine. Stir in oysters, cook for one minute or until oysters turn white and remove from heat.

To prepare patties:

- Roll out dough ⅛" thick on a lightly floured board.

- Cut into 2½" x 5" pieces.

- Place a little filling in the centre of each piece, fold over, moisten edges and press to seal.

- Heat oil or vanaspati in a deep frying pan. Lower

heat and deep fry patties 2 at a time, sealed side down, so that the 'leaves' open. Fry till pale gold in colour. Drain on paper towel.

To serve:

- Arrange warm patties on a platter garnish with sprigs of parsley, celery and fresh coriander.

Note: The oil must not be too hot or the layers will not separate, and the patties may remain raw inside though brown on the outside. Tongs help control the position of the patties while frying.

FORMINHAS COM MEXILHÕES
Mussel Tartlets

Makes: 18-20 tartlets

This is a particularly dainty party snack. The trick is to make the pastry thin enough to melt in the mouth, crisp enough to be interesting and firm enough not to disintegrate when held in the hand.

You will need tartlet trays for this dish—each tartlet about 1½" wide across the top.

Pastry:

1½ cup refined flour (maida)
Salt to taste
½ tsp chilli powder
¾ cup shortening
Cold water to mix

Oil for greasing tartlet moulds

Filling:

1½ cup shelled mussels, cleaned
1 tbsp oil
1 large onion, chopped
2 green chillies, deseeded and slit
6 large cloves garlic, finely minced
2 tbsp white wine
Salt to taste

Sauce:

1 hard-boiled egg
4 tbsp olive oil

½ tsp sugar
Salt to taste
½ tsp vinegar

Garnish:

10 olives, sliced

Pastry:

- Sift flour, salt and chilli powder together.

- Mix flour with shortening in a bowl till it resembles breadcrumbs. Add enough cold water to form a firm dough. Knead well.

- Roll out dough ⅛" thin on lightly floured board. Cut out circles, 2" in diameter, with a wineglass and press into lightly greased tartlet moulds.

- Prick base of pastry with a fork, and bake in a preheated oven at 175°C (350°F) for 20-30 minutes till golden brown.

- Carefully remove from moulds and allow to cool.

Filling:

- Heat oil in a pan and fry onion till opaque. Add chilli and garlic. Fry for one minute. Stir in wine.

- Reduce heat to low and cook pressing onion with back of spoon till reduced to a thick sauce.

- Add mussels and salt and cook for 2 minutes. Remove chillies and set aside to cool. The mixture should be moist.

Sauce:

- Separate yolk and white of egg.

- Mash yolk with olive oil, sugar and salt to a smooth paste. Slowly add vinegar, mixing all the while.

To *prepare tartlets*:

- Stir sauce into mussel mixture.

- Fill into pastry shells, making sure of at least one mussel per shell.

- Garnish with chopped egg white and sliced olives.

EMPADINHAS
Little Pork Pies

Makes: 24-30 pies

The contrast of sweet pastry and spicy filling is perfect, but certainly not meant for calorie watchers. The pies keep for a week—if they last that long!

You will need tartlet trays for this dish.

Pastry:
¼ kg (1¼ cup) sugar
2-3 tbsp lard, margarine or ghee (clarified butter)
Yolk of 9 large eggs
½ tsp salt
¾ kg (5 cups) fine semolina (rava)

Oil for greasing tartlet moulds
Egg white for brushing tops of tartlets

Filling:
¾ kg pork, preferably belly cut, chopped into tiny cubes
2 tbsp oil
4 medium onions, finely chopped
1½" piece ginger, ground
10-12 cloves garlic, finely sliced
1½ tsp turmeric powder
1½ tsp cumin powder
10 green chillies, finely chopped
Salt to taste
2 tbsp vinegar
2 tbsp feni (optional)

Finely ground:

10 cloves
2" piece cinnamon
10 peppercorns

Garnish:

Shredded lettuce or cabbage leaves

Pastry:

- Beat fat and sugar together till creamy.

- Add yolks and salt and continue beating till frothy.

- Add semolina, a spoonful at a time, mixing well.

- Turn onto board and knead thoroughly to achieve a pliable dough. Let dough rest, covered, for an hour.

Filling:

- Wash pork and pat dry.

- Heat oil in a pan and fry onions till golden. Add ginger, garlic and finely ground spices. Fry for one minute.

- Add turmeric, cumin powder and chillies.

- Add pork and salt to taste. Mix thoroughly.

- Cook over low heat, stirring occasionally. Add minimum water if necessary, until meat is cooked. The mixture should be moist.

- Add vinegar and feni, if using. Correct seasoning.

- Let mixture cool.

To prepare tartlets:

- Lightly grease moulds.

- Divide dough into balls, one for each tartlet mould.

- Reserve a little dough for the lid and press remaining dough into each mould to line.

- Fill cooled mixture into prepared moulds. Flatten each piece of reserved dough to form a lid. Cover moulds, moistening edges to seal. Make two cuts in each lid.

- Brush each pie with a little egg white.

- Bake in a preheated oven at 175°C (350°F) till golden brown, about ¾ hour.

- Remove from moulds and serve warm on a platter or tray surrounded with finely shredded lettuce or cabbage leaves.

PASTEIS FAVORITOS
Favourite Patties

Makes: 15-18 patties

This recipe is a favourite both with the cook, because it is simple and quick to make, and with those lucky enough to savour them. If served for a party, a daintier version could use a wineglass for cutter.

Filling:

¼ kg ground beef
1 large onion, finely minced
5 cloves garlic, finely minced
½" piece ginger, finely minced
3 green chillies, deseeded and finely minced
8 peppercorns, ground
1 tbsp vinegar
½ tsp sugar
1 tsp cumin powder
Salt to taste

Dough:

¾ kg (6 cups) refined flour (maida)
½ tsp salt
1½ tbsp shortening or oil
Water to mix

Oil for deep frying

Filling:

- Place all ingredients in pressure cooker with one cup water and cook for about 20 minutes.

- Let cooker cool.
- The mixture should be moist and not too dry. Either dry off excess liquid or add a little water. Adjust seasoning and let mixture cool.

Dough:

- Blend flour with salt, shortening and enough water to make a firm dough. Knead well.

To *prepare patties*:

- Roll out dough ⅛" thick and stamp out rounds about 2½" in diameter.
- Place a little mixture at centre of one round, moisten edges, place second round on top, and press to seal using tines of a fork. Make remaining patties in the same way.
- Heat oil in a deep frying pan. Deep fry patties over medium heat till golden brown.
- Drain on paper towel and serve hot.

CROQUETTES
Rissoles

Makes: 18-20 croquettes

Dainty cylinder-shaped rissoles delicately flavoured make a perfect accompaniment to any alcoholic drink.

½ kg leftover roast beef, minced
1 large egg, beaten
1 medium onion, finely chopped
½ tsp pepper powder
½ tsp nutmeg powder
1 tsp sugar
1 tbsp vinegar
Salt to taste
Fine breadcrumbs or semolina (rava) for coating
Oil for shallow frying

- Beat egg and combine with remaining ingredients except breadcrumbs and oil. Leave for one hour for flavours to meld.

- Mix again. Form into cocktail-sausage size rolls, coat with breadcrumbs or fine semolina.

- Heat oil in a frying pan and shallow fry croquettes till golden brown. Drain on paper and serve hot, skewered with toothpicks.

Appetizers

PÃO COM CHOURIÇO
Goa Sausage Burgers

Makes: 6 burgers

The well-loved Goa sausage in a particularly appealing presentation! It is easy and quick to make.

Small bread loaves in Goa have a slightly crusty outside and a soft inside.

2 Goa sausages, 4" in size
6 small loaves of bread, lightly toasted
1 medium onion, finely sliced
Chopped coriander leaves (optional)

- Place sausages and enough water to cover in a pan. Cook over medium heat for 10-15 minutes, till fairly dry. There should be about 2 tablespoons of liquid left.

- Allow to cool. Cut open and mash filling with back of spoon, keeping it moist.

- Split loaves, spread with sausage meat, sliced onion and coriander leaves.

- Alternately, split loaves and toast under grill, spread each half with sausage meat, sliced onion and coriander leaves.

BOJE
Nuggets of Bengal Gram

Serves: 3-4

The vendor of these tasty titbits sets up shop outside the village taverna and does brisk business with his piping hot boje, spiced with chilli and ginger. At social events, the boje achieves elegance when skewered on toothpicks and served with a tomato sauce dip.

1 cup Bengal gram (channa dal), washed and soaked for 12 hours
1" piece ginger, finely minced
1 medium onion, finely minced
3 green chillies, deseeded and finely minced
1 tsp coriander seeds, ground
1 tbsp chopped fresh coriander leaves
1 tsp baking powder
¼ fresh coconut, finely chopped (optional)
Salt to taste
Oil for deep frying

- Grind soaked dal coarsely. Mix in remaining ingredients except oil. The mixture should be of dropping consistency.

- Heat oil in deep frying pan. Using 2 teaspoons, drop in nuggets of mixture and deep fry over medium heat till golden brown.

- Drain on paper and serve hot.

- A mixture of tomato and chilli sauce makes a good dip.

Soups

Soup was definitely a Portuguese legacy, alien to the Goan palate to begin with. However, the Goans became so fond of it that soon every household had a stockpot simmering at the corner of the chulha. Into it went trimmings and bones of meat, chicken and vegetable parings. To it was added bits of turmeric, coriander seeds, ginger and whole spices. So in no time at all, the housewife could use the rich stock to produce a bowl of fragrant delicious soup for a visitor.

SOPA DE CAMARÃO
Prawn Soup

Serves: 6

Prawns sold in Goa are so fresh that a cloth has to be tied over the basket to keep them from jumping out. The frugal housewife uses the shells and heads of the prawns to make a rich stock. The prawns are washed well before they are shelled.

Stock:
Heads and shells of ¾ kg fresh prawn, cleaned
1 onion, chopped
1 tomato, chopped
¼" piece ginger, finely sliced
1 tsp whole coriander seeds
½ tsp turmeric powder
8-10 peppercorns
8 cups water
Salt to taste

Soup:

½ cup shelled prawns, cleaned and deveined
1 tbsp oil
1 medium onion, finely sliced
½ cup finely diced potato
Salt and pepper to taste

Garnish:

Finely chopped coriander leaves
Sliced celery

Stock:

- Roast heads and shells of prawns in a toaster oven or roast on tava or griddle till red in colour. Put into a large pan, with remaining ingredients.

- Bring to boil and simmer till reduced to 6 cups.

- Strain and keep aside.

Soup:

- Chop prawns if large.

- Heat oil in a pan and fry onion till golden. Add potato and fry for 2 minutes.

- Add stock, bring to boil then simmer till potato is done. Add prawns, cook for 2 minutes and remove from heat. Add salt and pepper to taste.

- Serve sprinkled with coriander leaves or celery.

SOPA DE CAMARÃO E BATATA
Prawn Soup with Potatoes

Serves: 6

1 cup shelled prawns, cleaned, deveined and lightly salted
3 onions, chopped
4 medium potatoes, cubed
4 cups stock made with shells of prawns as in previous recipe
1 cup milk
2 eggs yolks
1 tbsp butter
Salt to taste
Fresh coriander leaves or bread croutons for garnish

- Chop prawns if large.

- Boil onions and potatoes in stock till soft. Pass through a sieve or purée in a blender.

- Mix egg yolks with milk.

- Place purée in a pan and warm gently. Slowly stir in milk mixture and butter. Do not let soup go beyond a simmer.

- Add prawns and cook till they curl up.

- Adjust seasoning and add enough stock or water to make 6 cups. The soup should not be too thick.

- Garnish with a few coriander leaves or serve with bread croutons.

CALDO DE GALINHA
Chicken Broth

Serves: 6

This broth is light yet, nourishing and easily digested. It is made for small children, convalescents, invalids and the elderly.

The chicken in Goa are free-ranging in the villages and so are more flavoursome than their broiler battery-bred cousins.

1 chicken
1 medium onion, sliced
1 medium tomato, sliced
¼" piece ginger, sliced
1" piece cinnamon
3 cloves
8 peppercorns
1 tsp whole coriander seeds
½ tsp turmeric powder
½ tbsp olive oil (optional)
Salt to taste
Coriander leaves for garnish

- Wash and chop chicken into large pieces. Remove skin if desired. Reserve heart, liver and gizzard.

- Put 8 cups water in a large pan with all ingredients except olive oil. Bring to boil, lower heat and simmer till reduced to 6 cups.

- Strain.

- Add salt and olive oil.

- Serve garnished with coriander leaves.

Note: To make a richer soup, add raw chopped liver, gizzard and heart, after stock has been brought to boil. Shredded cooked chicken may also be added.

SOPA GROSSA
Minestrone – Goan Style

Serves: 4-6

Sopa Grossa is a very sustaining soup, thick with finely chopped vegetables, pasta and slivers of meat; it is usually served with small crusty loaves of bread and is a meal in itself.

1 medium onion, finely sliced
1 tbsp oil for frying
1 tomato, chopped
1 tbsp fine white rice
½ cup macaroni or shell pasta
8 cups chicken or meat stock, or equivalent from cubes
2 cups finely sliced carrots, French beans, cabbage, potatoes and cauliflower, and green peas
Salt and pepper to taste
½ cup shredded cooked chicken
½ cup cubed ham
2 celery stalks, 6" each, chopped (optional)
½ tbsp olive oil

- Heat oil for frying in a pan and fry onions till brown.

- Add tomato and cook for 2 minutes.

- Add rice and pasta and fry for one minute.

- Add half the stock. Simmer till rice and pasta are half cooked.

- Add vegetables, salt, pepper and remaining stock. Bring to boil. Lower heat and simmer till vegetables, rice and pasta are done.

- Add chicken, ham and celery. Cook for 2 minutes. Add olive oil. Adjust seasoning.

- Stir and serve hot.

CALDO VERDE
Spinach Soup

Serves: 6

While vegetables are rather conspicuous by their absence in the Goan diet, a vegetable soup like this is very much appreciated.

The Potuguese recipe uses a green cabbage-like vegetable called couve.

400 gm spinach, washed and chopped
2 medium onions, finely sliced
4 cloves garlic, finely sliced
1½ cup milk
1½ cup water
1 tbsp butter
2 bouillon cubes (optional)
¼ tsp grated nutmeg
Salt and pepper to taste
Bread croutons or cream for garnish

- Put spinach, onion and garlic in a pan, cover and cook over low heat till onions turn opaque. Remove from heat and cool. Purée in a blender.

- Return to pan, add milk and water. Bring to boil then simmer for 5 minutes. Add more milk or water to obtain desired consistency.

- Add butter, bouillon cubes, grated nutmeg, salt and pepper. Stir and cook for a further 5 minutes.

- Serve hot with croutons or a swirl of cream.

SOPA DE REPOLHO
Cabbage Soup

Serves: 6

Before refrigerators came to the village, the long-lasting cabbage was the stalwart stand-by vegetable. It is very versatile and can be shredded in a salad, cooked with prawns as a side-dish, or made into this delectable soup. The Portuguese olive oil imparts a special flavour, giving the soup 'personality', but butter is a good substitute.

¼ kg cabbage, washed and coarsely chopped
¼ kg (4 medium) onions, chopped
¼ kg (2 medium) potatoes, peeled and chopped
6 cups chicken or beef stock
Salt and pepper to taste
1 cup milk
1 tbsp Portuguese olive oil or butter
1 cup grated cheese

- Place all ingredients except oil, cheese and milk in a large pan. Bring to boil, then simmer till vegetables are tender.

- When cool, process in blender or pass through sieve.

- Return to pan and add milk. If too thick, stir in more stock or milk. Adjust seasoning. Heat through and stir in oil or butter.

- Sprinkle with grated cheese and serve hot.

Fish

With such a wide variety of fish—from whitebait to wiswond, and such an abundance of shellfish and crustaceans, it is little wonder that fish in some form is a 'must' at every Goan meal.

Before the advent of the Portuguese, Goans certainly cooked fish in many guises but they eagerly added Portuguese fish pies and stews to their repertoire, adapting them of course to their own palates.

CALDINHO
Mild Fish Curry

Serves: 6-8

Mild enough for children to enjoy, a caldinho tastes best made with small, fresh mullet, but any white fish will do.

Basic curry masala:

1 coconut, grated
½" piece ginger
1 tsp coriander seeds
8 peppercorns
2 green chillies, deseeded if desired
8 cloves garlic
½ tsp turmeric powder
1 tsp rice

Caldinho:

1 tbsp oil
1 medium onion, sliced
Pulp from tamarind the size of a walnut, soaked in ½ cup warm water
2-3 cloves, powdered

½" piece cinnamon, powdered
½ kg fish, sliced and lightly salted
Salt to taste

- Grind ingredients for curry masala together coarsely with a little water.

- Squeeze the paste by hand over a strainer, to extract thick milk.

- Add one cup hot water to paste, mix well and squeeze again to extract thin milk in a separate container.

- Heat oil in a pan and fry onion till golden.

- Add thin milk from masala and allow to simmer. Add tamarind pulp and powdered spices. Cook for 5 minutes. Add fish and simmer till done, about 5 minutes more.

- Add thick milk from masala and salt to taste.

- Adjust seasoning.

- Serve with boiled rice.

Variation: **Caldinho de legumes (Mild vegetable curry):**
The basic curry can be turned into a vegetarian dish by substituting fish with slices of white pumpkin (petha) or marrow (ghia), or thick slices of fried aubergine.

CALDEIRADA
Mild Fish Curry

Serves: 2-3

A simple and easy to prepare dish, mild enough for children to enjoy, the recipe suits any white fish. Large fish like kingfish or salmon are cut into slices and the smaller ones like mullet, mackerel and sardines, cut in half or left whole.

To reduce the pungency, deseed the chillies or use capsicum instead.

6 slices large fish or 6 small, whole fish
Salt to taste
10 cloves garlic, minced
1" piece ginger, minced
4 green chillies, minced
¼ tsp turmeric powder
3 large onions, sliced into rounds
3 large tomatoes, sliced into rounds
1 tbsp vinegar
2 tbsp olive oil
Chopped coriander leaves for garnish

- Clean and wash fish. Apply a little salt and keep aside for half an hour.

- Mix, garlic, ginger, green chillies, turmeric powder and a little salt.

- In a shallow pan, arrange half the onions in a layer, followed by half the tomatoes. Place half the fish on top and sprinkle with half spice mixture. Repeat

layers with remaining ingredients. Pour over
vinegar,   oil   and   one   cup   water.

- Cover pan, place on medium heat and cook till fish
  is done. Shake and tilt pan, during the cooking
  process to prevent contents from sticking.

- Carefully lift out fish and arrange on serving dish.
  Pour over gravy, garnish with coriander leaves and
  serve.

CARIL DE PEIXE
Fish Curry

Serves: 4

This is pure Goan soul food! Perfect eaten with nutty-flavoured thick red Goa rice, accompanied by crisp fried small fish or prawns.

Almost any fish tastes good in this curry, which amazingly tastes better the next day.

As alternatives to tamarind, slivers of fresh or dried raw mango, dried kokum, or 'bimblee' fresh or dried may be added. If the fish used is an oily sea fish—mackerel, sardines or surmai—then small lemon flavoured berries called tefla are added.

½ kg fish, sliced and lightly salted.
1 onion, sliced
Pulp from tamarind the size of a walnut soaked in 1 cup water
2-3 green chillies, slit (optional)
Salt to taste

Finely ground with a little water:
8 dried red Kashmiri chillies
10 cloves garlic
8 peppercorns
1 tsp coriander seeds
½ coconut, grated
1 tsp turmeric powder

• Place ground spices in a pan with 2 cups water and sliced onion. Bring to boil, reduce heat and simmer. Cook for about 30 minutes, keeping liquid level constant by adding tamarind pulp. If other souring agents are used instead of tamarind, then add to pan with spices and adjust liquid with plain water.

- Add fish, bring to boil, reduce heat and simmer. Add slit green chillies for added pungency. Cook for 5 minutes. Adjust seasoning and remove from heat.

- Serve with boiled rice and crisp fried small fish or prawns.

AMBOT-TIK
Hot and Sour Fish Curry

Serves: 4

A hot-sour curry made with any coarse fish—skate, baby shark or catfish and without coconut, so cholesterol watchers can enjoy it without a care. Indeed, it is difficult to stop eating it, so seductive is the flavour!

Skate and shark should be skinned and cut into cubes. Catfish should be sliced.

½ kg fish
1½ tbsp oil
1 medium onion, sliced
1 cup water
Pulp from tamarind the size of a walnut soaked in 1 cup water
A few dried kokum or dried mango slices
Salt to taste
Vinegar to taste

Finely ground with a little vinegar:
8 dried red Kashmiri chillies
6 peppercorns
6 cloves garlic
1 tsp turmeric powder
½" piece ginger
½ tsp cumin seeds

- Heat oil in a pan and fry onion till brown. Add ground masala, water and tamarind pulp. Simmer on low heat for about 10 minutes. Bring to boil and add kokum and salt.

- Add fish and lower heat. Simmer till done. Adjust seasoning and add vinegar if desired.

- Serve with plain boiled rice.

PEIXE À PORTUGUESA
Fish—Portuguese Style

Serves: 4

This is called 'Portuguese' because of the presence of olive oil. The mild flavour of the dish allows one to appreciate the freshness and flavour of the fish, while the spices make it very Goan in character.

Any white fish like kingfish (surmai) or salmon (rawas) may be used.

½ kg fish, sliced, washed and lightly salted
1 large onion, sliced in rings
2 tomatoes, sliced in rounds
½" piece ginger, finely chopped
4 cloves garlic, finely chopped
2 green chillies, slit and deseeded if desired
1 cup water
2 tbsp Portuguese olive oil or any salad oil
Vinegar to taste
Salt to taste
Chopped coriander leaves for garnish

- Place a layer of onions and tomatoes in a large flat pan. Sprinkle on ginger, garlic and green chillies. Add water. Cover and cook on medium heat till onions are opaque.

- Add olive oil and place fish carefully in a layer in pan. Cover and cook for 2 minutes. Carefully turn fish with a spatula, cover and cook for another 2 minutes.

- Add vinegar and salt.
- Serve hot, garnished with chopped coriander leaves.

BARRADA DE PEIXE
Curried Fish—Daman Style

Serves: 6-8

The people of the small erstwhile Portuguese enclave of Daman devised this way of cooking fish. The aniseed (saunf) gives it a Gujarati character, rather pleasing to the palate.

1½ kg kingfish (surmai), sliced
Salt to taste
2 tbsp oil
4 onions, chopped
3 tomatoes, chopped
3 tbsp chopped fresh coriander leaves
1" piece ginger, sliced
½ tbsp tamarind pulp (optional)

Marinade:

8 dried red chillies
8 cloves garlic
1 tbsp coriander seeds
6 cloves
1 tsp aniseed (saunf)
1 tsp cumin powder
½ tsp peppercorn
1" piece whole turmeric

Garnish:

Chopped fresh coriander leaves

- Grind ingredients for marinade together.

- Apply a little salt and marinade to fish. Set aside for half an hour.

- Heat oil in a pan. Add onions and ginger and fry till onions are limp. Add tomatoes and coriander. Mix well. Add fish and cook on low heat for 3 minutes.

- Pour in ½ cup water and tamarind pulp. Stir and cook till done. Adjust seasoning.

- Carefully lift slices onto dish, spoon over gravy, and garnish with fresh coriander.

FRITADA DE PEIXE
Fried Fish in Gravy

Serves: 4-6

This dish is delicious eaten with chapatti and a fugad of cabbage.

¾ kg kingfish (surmai), sliced, washed and lightly salted
Flour for dusting fish
Oil to lightly fry fish
½ tsp turmeric powder
1 tsp cumin powder
1" piece cinnamon, powdered
6 cloves, powdered
2 tbsp oil
1 large onion, sliced
5 cloves garlic, ground
3 green chillies, slit
1½ tbsp vinegar
Salt to taste
Chopped fresh coriander leaves for garnish

- Dust fish with a little flour and fry lightly, not enough to cook through. Remove and set aside.

- Mix all masala powders with a little water.

- Heat 2 tablespoons oil in a pan. Fry onion and garlic lightly. Add masala paste and fry for 2 minutes.

- Stir in one cup water, green chillies and vinegar. Bring to boil, add fish and lower heat. Simmer till done. Adjust seasoning.

- Garnish with chopped coriander leaves and serve.

ALMONDEGAS DE PEIXE
Fish Cakes

Serves: 4-6

After the monsoon, there is usually a glut of bangdas, and the palate tires of facing them fried and curried. The lime juice and the green chillies in this recipe cut the richness of the fish.

½ kg fresh mackerel (bangdas)
Salt to taste
2 cloves garlic, ground
1 medium potato, thinly sliced
1 large onion, minced
6 green chillies, minced
1 large egg
1 tbsp chopped fresh coriander leaves
Juice of 1 lime
1 cup fine semolina (rava)
Oil for shallow frying

- Clean mackerel, remove heads and wash well. Salt lightly.

- Put 1½ cup water, garlic and potatoes in a pan and bring to boil. Add fish, lower heat and cook till done.

- Cool. Lift out fish and potato, mash together with onions, chillies, egg, fresh coriander and lime juice. Adjust seasoning.

- Shape mixture into cutlets. Heat oil in a frying pan, dredge cutlets with semolina and shallow fry.

- Serve hot.

FILETES ENROLADAS DE CAÇÃO OU RAIA
Rolled Fillet of Baby Shark or Skate Fish

Serves: 4

Since the main item of Goan diet is fish, it is fortunate that Goa enjoys a wide variety. Baby shark and skate are considered delicacies when cooked liked this. Garnished with match-stick potatoes, green peas and tomato wedges, it looks European and tastes Goan!

½ kg fillet of baby shark or skate fish
2 tbsp vinegar or lime juice
1 tsp salt
2 tbsp recheio masala
1 egg, beaten
Fine semolina (rava) or breadcrumbs for coating rolls
Oil for deep frying

- Sprinkle fish fillet with vinegar or lime juice and salt and leave to marinate for one hour.

- Apply recheio masala on one side of each fillet. Roll carefully inwards and secure with toothpicks.

- Heat oil in a deep frying pan. Dip fish rolls in beaten egg, roll in semolina or breadcrumbs and deep fry. Drain on paper towel.

- Remove toothpicks and serve hot.

PEIXE RECHEADO COM TEMPERO VERDE
Whole Fish With Green Masala

Serves: 6-8

This is my son Larry's speciality and a party star. Choose a firm-fleshed, bright-eyed fish like kingfish (surmai) or salmon (rawas) for this dish.

The traditional method uses banana leaves to wrap the fish, but aluminium foil serves as well.

1-1½ kg fish
Juice of 2-3 limes
Salt to taste
Green chutney made with ½ coconut (see recipe)
1-1½ cups oil
Foil for wrapping
Wedges of lime and tomato and sprigs of fresh coriander for garnish

- Wash and clean fish.

- With a sharp knife, slit fish along both sides of backbone as you would to fillet, but do not separate the pieces. With kitchen shears, cut away backbone and remove. Rinse well and rub with salt and lime juice.

- Pack fish with chutney.

- Lay foil on flat surface and spread generously with oil. Place fish on foil and pour a spoonful of oil over fish. Fold foil over fish and crimp to seal.

- Place fish on a baking tray and bake in preheated

oven at 200°C (400°F) for 30-45 minutes.

- Remove tray from oven and allow to rest for 10 minutes.

- Place fish on serving dish, and serve garnished with wedges of lime and tomato and sprigs of fresh coriander.

PEIXE SERRA TEMPERADO
Spiced Whole Kingfish

Serves: 6-8

1½ kg fresh kingfish (surmai)
2 tbsp oil
3 medium onions, chopped
4 large tomatoes, chopped
8 tbsp chopped fresh coriander leaves
1 tsp sugar
Juice of 2 large limes
Salt to taste

Finely ground in a little vinegar:
8 red or green chillies
5 cloves garlic
5 peppercorns
½ tsp cumin seeds
1" piece ginger

Garnish:

Tomato halves or potato wafers

- After grinding masala, rinse mixer or grinding stone with one cup water and retain water.

- Wash and clean fish. Slit along both sides of backbone as you would to fillet fish but do not separate the pieces. Rub with salt.

- Heat oil in a pan and fry onions till soft. Add ground masala and fry well. Stir in tomatoes, coriander leaves, sugar, lime juice and salt. Cook till dry enough to stuff fish.

- Add one teaspoon masala to reserved masala water. Stuff remaining masala into fish on both sides of backbone.

- Pour masala water into a baking dish and place fish on top. Bake in a preheated moderate oven at 190°C (375°F) for 30 minutes, basting frequently till done.

- Remove fish to a flat serving dish, garnish with tomato wedges or potato wafers and serve hot.

PEIXE RECHEADOS
Stuffed Fried Fish

Serves: 2

Almost any fish tastes good this way, especially mackerel with its strong flavour. Allow 1-2 mackerel per person or one medium pomfret for two.

3-4 mackerel or 1 medium pomfret
½ tsp salt
Juice of 1 lime
2 tbsp rechieo masala
Oil for shallow frying

- Clean and wash fish well. Make a slit along both sides of backbone almost across the fish, as you would to fillet, but do not separate the fish pieces. Apply salt and lime juice all over fish. Fill recheio masala inside slits, and tie together with string if fish is large.

- Heat oil in a frying pan and shallow fry fish over medium heat. Turn fish, twice to achieve a deep brown colour.

CAVALAS FUMADAS EM FENO
Smoked Mackerel

Serves: 5-6

A harvest time treat!

In Goa, the family gathers on the back veranda, plates ready to receive the steaming blackened fish. The skin is peeled away and the succulent flesh eaten with a squeeze of lime.

6-12 mackerel
1 tbsp cooking salt
Coarse brown sea-salt
Banana leaves to wrap fish
2-3 limes, sliced

- Clean and wash fish. Apply cooking salt in cavity. Coat outside of fish with coarse salt, pressing it into salt.

- Wrap fish in banana leaves. Place on a bed of hay in a single layer. Cover with more hay.

- Set hay on fire, putting on more hay as required, for about 15-20 minutes till fish is cooked.

- Remove fish with tongs, unwrap and serve with lime slices.

SALADA DE CÁVALAS SALGADAS
Salad of Salted Mackerel

Serves: 4

The largest, fattest mackerel are specially salted for salads. They remain soft and ooze fat. They are called 'salade bangdas'.

1 mackerel (salade bangda)
1 tbsp Goa palm vinegar
½ tsp sugar
Salt to taste
½ tbsp olive oil (optional)
2 large onions, finely chopped
1 large tomato, finely chopped
4 green chillies, finely chopped
1 tbsp chopped fresh coriander leaves

- Roast mackerel over embers only as excessive heat will leave it raw inside. Peel away skin, discard bones and shred flesh.

- Put vinegar, sugar, salt and olive oil in a jar. Shake well to mix.

- Place onions, tomatoes, chillies and shredded fish in a bowl. Pour over dressing and toss to mix. Adjust Seasoning.

- This preparation is usually served as an accompaniment to fish curry and rice, or with canji.

BACALHAU
Portuguese Salt Cod with Dried Beans

Serves: 4-6

A lot of people in Goa still get misty-eyed over bacalhau or Portuguese salt cod. It was cooked with rice, fried in fofos or cooked with dried beans as below. Now it has become a luxury, but salted ray or shark makes an acceptable substitute. Choose freshly salted, firm-fleshed dried fish.

This is a typical Portuguese recipe.

½ cup chick peas (kabuli channa)
¼ kg bacalhau, salted ray or shark
2 medium potatoes
½ cup macaroni
1½ tbsp olive oil
1 large onion, chopped
6 cloves garlic, chopped
3 cloves
1½" piece cinnamon
Salt to taste
Pepper to taste

- Wash chick peas and soak overnight.

- Place in pan with water and boil till tender. Drain and reserve water.

- Cut fish into pieces and soak in water for 2 hours. Drain fish and place in a pan with fresh water. Boil till tender. Allow to cool.

- Lift out fish and shred. Reserve water.

- Skin and cut potatoes into cubes. Place in a pan with water and boil till tender. Drain.

- Boil some salted water in a pan and cook macaroni in it till al dente. Drain.

- Heat half the oil in a pan and add onions, garlic, cloves and cinnamon. Fry for 2 minutes. Stir in chick peas, fish, potatoes and macaroni, adding just enough of the reserved liquids to give a thick gravy.

- Pour in remaining oil and mix well. Season to taste with salt and pepper and serve.

CARIL DE CAMARÃO
Prawn Curry

Serves: 6-8

In Goa, prawns are so flavoursome because they are very fresh. A Goan would be willing to pay well for fresh prawns rather than less for frozen or iced prawns.

There are almost as many recipes for prawn curry as there are cooks, but this is one of the simpler methods.

1 cup shelled prawns, cleaned, deveined and lightly salted
2½ cups milk extracted from 1 grated coconut, or ½ coconut ground to a paste
1 tsp coriander powder
2 tsp Kashmiri chilli powder
6 cloves garlic, ground
1 medium onion, finely sliced
2 green chillies, slit and deseeded
Salt to taste
Tamarind the size of a walnut, soaked in ½ cup water

- Put all ingredients except prawns and tamarind water into a pan with 2 cups water. Mix well.

- Bring to boil, reduce heat and simmer till onions turn soft. Stir occasionally.

- Squeeze tamarind and strain into pan. Stir in prawns. Adjust seasoning. Remove from heat as soon as prawns curl up.

Note: In season, sliced raw mango or bimblee are added instead of tamarind for an extra tart curry.

𝐂

CAMARÃO 'TIGRE' FRITO
Fried Tiger Prawns

Serves: 4-6

'Vagh' in Konkani means 'tiger', implying size, ferocity and stripes. This term very aptly describes these prawns which in the Goa region are a respectable eight inches long. This is a favourite family recipe.

8-10 large fresh tiger prawns
1" piece ginger
8 cloves garlic
3 green chillies, deseeded if desired
Salt to taste
2 tbsp feni
Flour for dredging
1 egg, beaten
Fine semolina (rava) or breadcrumbs for coating
Oil for shallow frying
Lime wedges for garnish

- Wash prawns well, shell and devein, leaving tail. Slit carefully and flatten with broad bladed knife.

- Grind ginger, garlic and chillies to a paste. Mix with salt and feni. Apply paste to both sides of prawns and leave to marinate for 30 minutes.

- Dredge each prawn with flour, dip in beaten egg, and coat with semolina or breadcrumbs. Heat oil in a frying pan. Shallow fry prawns till golden brown, on medium heat.

- Serve hot with wedges of lime.

CAMARÃO COM CEBOLAS
Prawns with Onions

Serves: 4-6

As good as this recipe looks, lessening or increasing the spices used, or not de-seeding the chillies varies the pungency of the dish.

It can be served as an accompaniment to rice and fish curry, as a snack on toast, or as a filling for pancakes, tartlets and omelets—a versatile recipe indeed, and easy to make as well.

1 cup shelled prawns, small to medium sized, cleaned, deveined and lightly salted
2 tbsp oil
3 large onions, finely sliced
6 cloves garlic, finely sliced
1" piece ginger, finely sliced
3 green chillies, deseeded and finely sliced
1 large tomato, skinned and chopped
½ tsp cumin powder
A dash of vinegar (Optional)
Salt to taste
1 tbsp chopped fresh coriander leaves

- Chop prawns if large.

- Heat oil in a pan and fry onions over medium heat till opaque.

- Stir in garlic, ginger and chillies and cook for 2 minutes.

- Add tomato and cumin powder and cook for 2

minutes, stirring to prevent sticking.

- Stir in prawns. Cook only till prawns turn pink and curl up. Add vinegar if using and adjust seasoning.

- Remove from heat, stir in coriander leaves and serve.

EMPADA DE CAMARÃO
Prawn Pie

Serves: 4-6

Under a demure pastry the filling is savoury—very Goan.
A surprise and delight.

Pastry:

1½ cup refined flour (maida)
A good pinch of chilli powder
Salt to taste
¾ cup shortening
A squeeze of lime
Milk to brush top of pie

Filling:

1½ cup very fresh shelled prawns, cleaned, deveined and lightly
salted (reserve heads and shells for stock)
2 tbsp oil
3 large onions, finely sliced
2 large tomatoes, skinned and chopped
1½ tbsp recheio masala
1 tsp sugar
½ tsp salt
2 tsp vinegar
1 tbsp chopped fresh coriander leaves
2 eggs, hard-boiled and sliced

Sauce:

Heads and shells of prawns
½ onion, chopped
½" slice ginger
1 bay leaf
1 tbsp oil

℃

117

1 tbsp refined flour (maida)
Salt to taste

Pastry:

- Sift flour, chilli powder and salt into a bowl.

- Cut in shortening and work lightly with hands till mixture resembles fine breadcrumbs.

- Add lime juice and enough water to make a firm dough. Knead well and set aside.

Filling:

- Heat oil in pan and fry onions over medium heat till opaque. Stir in tomatoes and cook for 2 minutes.

- Add masala, sugar, salt and vinegar. Stir to mix thoroughly.

- Stir in prawns and coriander leaves. Cook only till prawns curl up. Remove from heat. Adjust seasoning.

Sauce:

- Toast heads and shells of prawns in toaster oven or roast on tava or griddle till red.

- Place in a pan with 2 cups water, onion, ginger and bay leaf. Boil till water is reduced to one cup. Strain and cool.

- Heat oil in a pan and add flour. Cook over medium heat, for about 2 minutes till flour is pale gold.

- Pour in stock, stirring to prevent lumps. Cook till

sauce thickens. Remove from heat and add salt.

- Stir sauce into prawn mixture.

- Adjust seasoning.

To *prepare pie*:

- Roll out 2 rounds of pastry to fit a 9" pie dish.

- Grease pie dish and line with one round of pastry. Prick base well with fork.

- Fill with prawn mixture. Arrange egg slices on top. Cover with second round of pastry.

- Moisten edges of pastry and press to seal. With a sharp knife, make 2 slits in pastry cover.

- Brush with milk and bake in preheated oven at 175°C (350°F), for 30 minutes, till golden brown.

APA DE CAMARÃO - I
Prawn Cake

Serves: 8-10

Delicious, rich and definitely not for the cholesterol-shy, this party dish, elegant and aromatic, earns kudos for the chief cook.

Batter:
½ kg (2½ cups) parboiled Goa rice, washed and soaked overnight
1 coconut, grated
2 cups toddy
8 egg yolks, beaten
2 tbsp sugar
Salt to taste

Filling:
4 cups shelled prawns, cleaned and deveined
2 tbsp oil
10 medium onions, finely sliced
1 tsp salt
Thick milk from ½ coconut
3-4 tbsp sugar
Vinegar to taste

Finely ground in a little vinegar:
10-12 dried red Kashmiri chillies
8 cloves garlic
1" piece cinnamon
8 peppercorns
6-8 cloves
1" ginger

Garnish:

Tomatoes cut in wedges
Green peas

Batter:

- Grind rice and coconut separately, adding toddy as necessary. Mix together. Add egg yolks, sugar, salt and toddy if necessary to form a batter of dropping consistency. Set aside to rise for about 4-6 hours.

Filling:

- Heat oil in a pan and fry onions till brown. Add ground spices, stir and add prawns and salt. Add coconut milk, sugar and vinegar to taste. The prawn mixture should taste hot, sweet and slightly sour, to contrast with the toddy flavour of the batter.

To prepare pie:

- Grease a fairly deep 9" baking tin and dust with flour. Pour in half the batter, which should be bubbly by now. Spread on prawn mixture evenly and top with remaining batter.

- Bake in preheated oven at 190°C (375°F) for about 30 minutes, till brown and done. Test with skewer. It should come out clean.

- Turn out, garnish with green peas and wedges of tomatoes and serve hot.

APA DE CAMARÃO - II
Prawn cake
Serves: 8-10

Twin sister to the classic recipe, this modern adaptation tastes as good as it looks and is far less trouble to make.

Batter:

½ cup semolina (rava)
1 cup sugar
¾ cup butter
3 large eggs
1 tsp salt
2 cups refined flour (maida)
2 tsp baking powder
½ coconut, grated fine (reserve water from coconut)
½ cup milk
1 tsp vanilla or almond essence

Filling:

As for Apa de Camarão - I

Garnish:

Tomato wedges and sprigs of coriander

Batter:

- Soak semolina in coconut water.

- Cream sugar and butter together till light and fluffy. Beat in eggs one at a time. Stir in salt.

- Sift flour with baking powder and add to mixture alternately with coconut, semolina and milk. If necessary, add a little coconut water to obtain a batter of dropping consistency. Stir in essence.

To prepare pie:

- Prepare the apa in the same way as in previous recipe.
- Turn out, garnish with tomato wedges and coriander sprigs and serve warm.

XEQ XEQ
Thick Crayfish or Lobster Curry

Serves: 4

Though crabs or prawns taste good made this way, the thick curry of delicately balanced spices suits the crayfish best. Anyway, how much more exotic can you get than a lobster or crayfish dish that is spelt with an 'X'!

2 cups lobster or crayfish meat
1 coconut
1 tsp cumin seeds
4+1 cloves garlic
2 dried red chillies
1 tsp turmeric powder
18 peppercorns
1 tbsp oil
1 onion, finely sliced
1 green chilli, slit
¼" piece ginger, ground
Vinegar to taste
1 tsp salt

- Grind coconut, cumin seeds, 4 cloves garlic, red chillies, turmeric and peppercorns.

- Add ½ cup hot water to coconut paste, squeeze and strain milk. Add one more cup hot water to paste and squeeze thin milk into a separate container.

- Heat oil in a pan and sauté onion. Add slit green chilli, ginger and one clove ground garlic. Fry till onion is opaque.

- Add lobster meat and fry for 3 minutes more. Add thin coconut milk, vinegar and salt. Simmer for about 3 minutes. Add thick milk and simmer for a few minutes more.

- Adjust seasoning and serve.

CARIL DE CARANGUEJOS
Crab Curry

Serves: 4 - 6

There is a story about the people of Salcete that they never eat crabs at night because it takes time and lamps have to burn more oil at the dinner table!

Select crabs that are fresh and heavy, are rather than large. To make sure that crabs are fresh, buy them live.

6 medium sized crabs, about 1 kg
2" piece ginger, finely ground
10 cloves garlic, finely ground
1 tbsp chilli powder
1 tsp cumin powder
2 tbsp oil
3 medium onions, sliced
Pulp from tamarind the size of a large
walnut, soaked in 1 cup water
Salt to taste

- Wash crabs well and plunge into boiling water. Cook till red. Lift out of pan and allow to cool. Break off claws and legs, separate carapace or shell from body, remove apron and feathery gills from underside. Remove stomach from between eyes. Cut body in half.

- Mix ginger, garlic and powdered masalas with a little water to make a paste.

- Heat oil in a pan and fry onions till soft. Add masala paste and fry for 2 minutes, adding a little water to prevent sticking.

- Add tamarind pulp, salt and crabs. Stir and mix well.

- Add one cup water, reduce heat and simmer for about 20 minutes, till done.

- Adjust seasoning and serve.

CARANGUEJOS RECHEADOS
Stuffed Crab

Serves: 6

My good friend Tatiana has, I suspect, a very special arrangement with the fishermen under the Cortalim bridge, to send her only the freshest, heaviest crabs, full of lac or coral. On one occasion, she just boiled a basketful of crabs with a few chillies. We sat around the table, napkins under our chins, and got down to probing and sucking out every morsel of crabmeat, between sips of feni and lime juice. That's what Goa is about—enjoying soul food with good friends!

6 large live crabs
2 tbsp oil
2 medium onions, chopped
1" piece ginger, ground
6 cloves garlic, ground
2 green chillies, deseeded
2 cloves, powdered
Salt to taste
1 egg, beaten
1 tbsp breadcrumbs
1 tbsp chopped fresh coriander
3 tbsp semolina (rava)
Oil for shallow frying

- Wash crabs well. Plunge into boiling water and cook till red in colour. Lift out and allow to cool.

- Separate carapace or shell, clean, wash out and drain. Carefully remove apron and gills from underside and stomach from between eyes. Pick out as much meat as possible from the body. Crack claws, remove meat and chop.

- Heat 2 tablespoons oil in a pan and fry onions till opaque. Add ginger, garlic and chillies. Fry for one minute. Stir in crab meat and clove powder. Mix well. Add salt, egg, breadcrumbs and coriander leaves. Mix well. The mixture should not be too dry.

- Divide mixture between shells, fill and press down. Sprinkle thickly with semolina.

- Heat oil in a frying pan. Place crabs filled side down and shallow fry for 1-2 minutes till brown. You may dribble some oil over filling and brown in preheated oven at 190°C (375°F) for 5 minutes.

AMEIJOAS COM COCO
Clams with Coconut

Serves: 4-6

In season, clams are harvested at the mouths of tidal rivers during low tide and sold by the hundred.

Tight-shut, medium sized ones are best. Any naturally open clams should be discarded.

They are called tisrio in Konkani and make an excellent accompaniment to a bowl of peize.

100 clams
1 tbsp oil
2 large onions, finely sliced
½" piece ginger, ground
6-8 cloves garlic, ground
½ tsp turmeric powder
1 tsp coriander powder
4 green chillies, cut in strips
Salt to taste
½ fresh coconut, grated

- To prepare clams, wash several times in water to clean sand. With a sharp knife, prise open shell and discard empty half. Do not wash again or the flavour will be lost.

- Heat oil in a pan and fry onions till soft. Add ginger and garlic and fry for one minute.

- Stir in turmeric and coriander powder and add green chillies.

- Pour in ½ cup water and bring to boil. Add salt and

clams. Lower heat and cook for 5 minutes, stirring occasionally.

- Stir in grated coconut and cook till fairly dry.

- Adjust seasoning and serve.

EMPADA DE OSTRAS À TIA RUBERTINA
Tia Rubertina's Oyster Pie

Serves: 6-8

This elaborate pie is a perfect blend of Goan and Portuguese culinary art and one of the classic dishes of Goan haute cuisine. The semolina has to absorb the lard, which requires patient kneading till the dough is pliable, not brittle.

Filling:

3 cups large fresh shelled oysters
2 tbsp olive oil
6 onions, cut in fine rings
1 large green chilli, finely chopped
½ tsp finely chopped ginger
3 cloves garlic, chopped
½ tsp salt
1 wineglass (½ cup) white wine
3 hard boiled eggs, sliced
12 olives, sliced
2 large tomatoes, sliced
3 large potatoes, boiled and sliced

Finely ground:

6 peppercorns
6 cloves
2" piece cinnamon

Pastry:

6 egg yolks
½ cup sugar

450 gm (3 cups) fine semolina
1 nutmeg, grated
Salt to taste
¾ cup lard or oil

Filling:

- Heat oil in a pan. Add onions, green chilli, ginger and garlic and fry to a rich brown.

- Add salt and ground spices and cook for 5 minutes. Stir to keep from sticking. Add wine. Cook till a thick gravy forms. Add oysters and cook for 2 minutes more.

- Adjust seasoning.

Pastry:

- Beat sugar and eggs yolks till light and fluffy.

- Sieve semolina into mixture and add grated nutmeg and salt. Mix well. Knead, adding enough lard to get a firm but pliable dough.

- Roll out two circles of pastry, ⅛" thick to line and cover a 9" baking dish. Prick over with a fork.

- Place a circle of pastry in the greased baking dish. Place a layer of oyster mixture, cover with half eggs, olives, tomatoes and potatoes. Add remaining oyster mixture, top with remaining eggs, olives, etc. Cover with second circle of pastry. Pinch edges to seal. Make three cuts in top of pie. Bake at 190°C (375°F) for 30-45 minutes till golden brown and serve.

LULAS GUIZADAS DO ALGARVE
Curried Squid a la Algarve

Serves: 6-8

This is a Portuguese recipe, definitely Mediterranean with the tomatoes and capsicum and does well on a party table.

1 kg squid, cleaned
6 medium onions
6 large tomatoes
4-6 capsicums
2 bouillon cubes
2 tbsp chopped fresh coriander
Salt to taste
1 tbsp chilli powder
½ cup cream
Chopped fresh coriander leaves for garnish

- Wash squid well and cut in strips.

- Mince onions. Peel, deseed and chop tomatoes. Remove seeds and white pith of capsicums and chop.

- Place squid, onions, tomatoes, and capsicum in a large pan. Sprinkle over crumbled bouillon cubes and salt and mix well.

- Allow squid to cook on low heat for 2 hours, adding water if necessary. When gravy is thick and squid cooked, stir in cream gently but thoroughly.

- Carefully lift slices onto dish, spoon over gravy, and garnish with fresh coriander. Serve with boiled white rice.

LULAS RECHEADAS
Stuffed Squid

Serves: 4-6

6 medium squid, cleaned
2 tbsp oil
4 large onions, chopped
3 large tomatoes, chopped
2 tbsp recheio masala
¾ tsp salt
Semolina (rava) or fine breadcrumbs for coating squid
Oil for shallow frying
Chopped fresh coriander leaves for garnish

- Chop tentacles of squid.

- Heat 2 tablespoons oil in a pan and fry onions till soft.

- Add tomatoes and masala. Stir well.

- Add chopped tentacles of squid and ½ cup water. Cook over medium heat till tender and fairly dry. Add salt and adjust seasoning.

- Fill mixture into squid pockets and pin closed with toothpicks

- Press stuffed squid into semolina or breadcrumbs to coat.

- Heat oil in a frying pan and shallow fry squid till golden brown.

- Serve warm garnished with fresh coriander.

Chicken

Every house, humble or exalted, had in the old days a few chicken scratching in the backyard. They were mostly fed leftover rice and ranged freely, sometimes invading the kitchen. The eggs they laid were small but very tasty. The chicken were lean with very little fat, but slow cooking rendered them tender.

ESTEW À MARIA FELICIA
Maria Felicia's Chicken Stew

Serves: 6-8

Actually a mild curry, this stew is a favourite with children and adults. It is served with oddé or rice.

1 kg chicken
Salt to taste
1 tbsp oil
2 medium onions, finely sliced
1" piece ginger, ground
6 cloves garlic, ground
4 green chillies, chopped
1 tsp turmeric powder
¾ tsp cumin powder
2 tsp coriander powder
Pulp from tamarind the size of a walnut, soaked in ½ cup water
2-3 boiled potatoes (optional)

Finely ground:

4 cloves
1½" piece cinnamon
Seeds of 3 green cardamoms
8 peppercorns

℃

139

- Wash and skin chicken, cut into pieces and salt lightly.

- Heat oil in a pan and fry onions till golden brown. Add ginger, garlic and chillies and fry for a minute.

- Add turmeric, cumin and coriander powders. If mixture is too dry, put in a spoonful of water. Stir well to mix.

- Put in chicken pieces and turn to cover with masala. Sprinkle over ground spices. Cover and cook over low heat, stirring occasionally. A little water may be added if needed.

- When chicken is cooked, add tamarind pulp. Stir well and adjust seasoning.

- Add potatoes if using, stir well and serve hot with rice or oddé.

CARIL DE GALINHA
Chicken Curry

Serves: 6-8

There are almost as many recipes for chicken curry, as there are families in Goa. The basic recipe is varied with balance of spices—some like it hot, other prefer it mild, increasing the chillies or coconut to their taste.

1 kg chicken, cut in pieces, lightly salted
1 large coconut
1 tbsp raw rice
8 cloves garlic
10 dried red Kashmiri chillies
½ tbsp cumin seeds
1" piece ginger
1 tsp coriander seeds
1 tbsp poppy seeds
4 green chillies
1 tbsp turmeric powder
2 tbsp oil
2 medium onions, finely sliced
Pulp from tamarind the size of a marble soaked in 1 cup water
Salt to taste

- Grate half coconut and grind coarsely with raw rice. Extract about ¾ cup thick milk and one cup thin milk.

- Grind remaining coconut with garlic and all dry spices.

- Heat oil in a pan and fry onions till golden brown. Add ground spices and fry over medium heat, stirring constantly, till oil rises to top.

- Add chicken and turn to coat all pieces with spices. Add thin coconut milk and salt and reduce heat. Simmer and cook till almost done.

- Add tamarind pulp and thick coconut milk. Cook till chicken is done.

- Serve with boiled rice.

XACUTI DE GALINHA
Chicken Curry

Serves: 6-8

Hindu Goans cook this to perfection. It was usually the
fate of the tough old rooster to appear on the table in this
guise, and the cooking was a patient, long process, but the
resultant curry was delectable.

Modern broilers cook faster.

1 kg chicken, cut into 8 pieces, lightly salted
1 large coconut
Tamarind the size of a walnut
1 tbsp dill (sua) seeds
2" piece cinnamon
12 peppercorns
1 tsp poppy seeds
2 large dried red chillies
1 tsp cumin seeds
1 tsp coriander seeds
1 tsp mustard seeds
1" piece ginger
2 tsp turmeric powder
2 tbsp oil
2 large onions, finely sliced
4 cloves garlic, finely sliced
6 cloves
6 green cardamoms
1 tbsp vinegar
Salt to taste
A pinch of grated nutmeg
Tiny cubes or slivers of coconut for garnish

- Grate coconut. Grind ¾ coarsely and extract thick and thin milk. Soak tamarind in thin coconut milk. Roast ¼ coconut on a tava or griddle till pale brown and aromatic.

- Roast next 8 ingredients, individually on a tava or griddle, add to roasted coconut and grind to a paste with ginger and turmeric powder.

- Heat oil in a pan and fry onions and garlic till brown. Add ground paste and fry for one minute.

- Add chicken, mix well and cook, covered till the chicken releases water. Squeeze out pulp from tamarind, add to curry and cook till chicken is almost done.

- Add thick coconut milk, cloves, cardamoms, vinegar and salt.

- Garnish with tiny cubes or slivers of coconut, sprinkle with grated nutmeg and serve with boiled rice.

GALINHA À ALZIRA
Alzira's Chicken

Serves: 4-6

A mild combination of chillies, vinegar and sugar gives this dish an intriguing flavour. It is a colourful dish that can be 'dressed up' for a party with green peas or rings of capsicum. The addition of sultanas and cashew nuts makes it 'royal'.

1 medium chicken cut into pieces
1½ tbsp ghee (clarified butter) or cooking oil
4 large onions, finely sliced
¼ kg (5 medium) tomatoes, chopped
½ tbsp vinegar
Salt to taste
Sugar to taste

Finely ground:
8 dried red Kashmiri chillies, deseeded
1 tsp turmeric powder
8 cloves garlic

- Heat ghee or oil in a pan and fry onions till soft. Add tomatoes and ground masala. Fry for 2 minute. Add chicken and continue frying till dry.

- Add sufficient hot water to cook chicken till tender.

- Add vinegar, salt and sugar. The taste should be hot, sweet and sour. The gravy should be thick and tomato-red in colour.

- Pour into a dish and serve.

𝕮

FRANGO VERA
Chicken Vera

Serves: 4

Spring chicken with just a hint of spice, crisp and succulent, cooked in a heavy skillet, taste best when eaten with fingers! I first enjoyed this dish at Vera's who then cooked it for us on many subsequent occasions.

2 spring chicken, preferably with skin, split in 2
½ tbsp recheio masala
1 tbsp turmeric powder
Salt to taste
Juice of 1 sour lime or 1 tbsp vinegar
1-2 tbsp oil
Sprigs of coriander leaves for garnish

- Wash chicken carefully and pat dry, Rub with masala, turmeric powder and salt, sprinkle with lime juice or vinegar and leave to marinate for one hour, turning once.

- Heat oil in a heavy bottomed pan, put in chicken taking care not to overlap pieces. Place a metal plate over chicken and weigh down with a heavy object. Cook on medium heat for 8-10 minutes. Uncover, turn chicken over, replace heavy cover and cook for a further 8-10 minutes. Make sure chicken does not burn. Pierce chicken with a skewer to test if done. The juice should be colourless.

- Serve garnished with sprigs of fresh coriander.

GALINHA PICANTE À ANGELA MERICIA
Spicy Chicken a la Angela Mericia

Serves: 6-8

This dish is really easy to make! Served with matchstick potatoes and green peas, or surrounding a Portuguese style pulau, it does a festive table proud.

1 chicken, 1½ kg in weight or 4 breasts of chicken
1½ tbsp recheio masala
1 tbsp vinegar or lime juice
2 tbsp oil
Salt to taste
1 tbsp feni

- Wash chicken and if using whole chicken, cut into eight pieces.

- Mix masala, vinegar or lime juice, oil and salt.

- Coat chicken pieces well with masala mixture, place in a ceramic dish and marinate for one hour.

- Arrange chicken in baking dish, spoon over feni and any remaining marinade. Cover dish with foil.

- Bake in a preheated oven at 190°C (375°F) for 15 minutes. Turn and baste chicken, cover and return to oven. Bake for 15 minutes more till done.

- Remove foil, place under grill to crisp meat and serve.

ASSADO DE GALINHA COM CHOURIÇO DE REINO
Roast Chicken with Portuguese Sausage

Serves: 6

Sausages made with wine, feni and olive oil have a delicate flavour and make an interesting version of stuffing for roast chicken.

1 chicken broiler with skin, about 1½ kg
1½ tsp salt
8 peppercorns, powdered
3 cloves garlic, finely ground
1 tbsp butter
Oil for basting

Stuffing:

1 chouriço de reino, 6" sausage
½ tbsp oil
2 medium onions, chopped
6 cloves garlic, sliced
3 green chillies, deseeded and sliced
Chicken giblets, finely chopped
3-4 slices bread
8-10 walnuts, chopped
6 peppercorns, powdered
Salt to taste

Stuffing:

- Boil sausage in 1½ cup water for about 10-15 minutes, till cooked. Slit sausage, discard casing and chop meat fine. Reserve broth.

- Heat oil in a pan and fry onions till brown. Add garlic and chillies.

- Stir in any liquor left over from boiling the sausage or ½ cup water. Add giblets and cook on low heat till tender.

- Cut bread into small cubes and add to mixture. Stir in sausage meat, walnuts and powdered peppercorns. The mixture should be moist. Adjust seasoning and mix well.

To prepare chicken:

- Wash chicken thoroughly inside and out.

- Rub chicken, inside and outside with salt and pepper. Mix butter with garlic. Lift skin on breast and spread butter evenly underneath.

- Fill stuffing into chicken and stitch up opening. Truss chicken and place breast upwards in a baking tin. Bake in a preheated oven at 190°C (375°F) for 45 minutes till golden brown, basting with fat in pan and a little oil.

- Remove trussing and serve.

GALINHA CAFREAL
Chicken Barbecue

Serves: 3-4

A recipe for a barbecue that tastes best cooked over a wood fire. Perhaps this is the Goan cousin of tandoori chicken.

1 chicken broiler, just under 1 kg
1 tsp salt
1 sour lime
100-125 gm butter

Finely ground:

2" piece ginger
6 dried red Kashmiri chillies
3 peppercorns
1 pod garlic

- Remove innards of chicken including liver and gizzard. Wash well, rub inside, and out with salt and lime juice. Rub ground spices into chicken, inside and outside. Leave to marinate for one hour.

- Apply a thin coating of butter to outside of chicken and roast over wood or charcoal fire, basting with a little butter at a time till chicken is done.

- Alternately, the chicken may be cut into pieces and cooked in a heavy bottomed pan over low heat. Little or no water should be added, and a little less butter is required.

FRANGO VENECIANA
Chicken Venician

Serves: 4

This recipe is from the treasury of Anita's mother and certainly not for weight-watchers.

2 spring chicken
½ tsp salt
½ tsp pepper
½ litre stock
1 bay leaf (tej patta), broken into pieces
5 tbsp white wine or feni
4 tbsp butter
½ tbsp refined flour (maida)
1 cup grated cheese

- Split chicken down the back into 2 pieces each. Wash, pat dry and rub with salt and pepper.

- Place stock in a wide shallow pan and bring to boil. Add bay leaf, wine and 2 tablespoons butter. Lower heat and carefully place split chicken into pan with skin side up. Simmer till done, turning chicken once only.

- Remove bay leaf. Lift chicken onto serving dish.

- Mix flour with one tablespoon water and stir into stock. Add remaining butter and cook till gravy thickens. Adjust seasoning.

- Spoon gravy over chicken, sprinkle with cheese on top and bake in preheated oven at 190°C (375°F) for 10-15 minutes, till cheese melts and turns crisp.

- Serve with boiled carrots, beans and potatoes tossed in butter.

GALANTINE DE GALINHA
Galantine of Chicken

Serves: 8-10

This is a simpler version of the classic dish that requires the chicken to be de-boned, stuffed, rolled, steamed, sliced and only then set in aspic. Nevertheless, this version looks and tastes just as good.

½ kg chicken breasts
Salt and pepper to taste
1 green chilli, slit
4 cloves garlic
2 chouriço de reino sausage
3 tbsp gelatine
A few leaves celery
2 cubes chicken bouillon
White of 1 egg, lightly beaten
1 tbsp brandy (optional)
3 hard-boiled eggs, sliced
A few olives, sliced
¼ kg cooked ham, cut in cubes
Tomato wedges and sprigs of parsley for garnish

- Place chicken with 1½ cup water, salt, pepper, chilli and garlic in a pan and cook over medium heat till done. Drain and reserve liquid.

- Slice chicken breasts.

- Place sausage in a pan with 1½ cup water and cook over medium heat, for about 10-15 minutes, till done. Drain and reserve liquid.

- Remove skin of sausage and chop meat.

- Soak gelatine in 1½ cup water for 30 minutes.

- Put celery leaves in a pan with 5 cups water and bring to boil. Add chicken cubes, salt and reserved liquids from chicken and sausages.

- Lower heat and simmer for 5-10 minutes. Bring to boil and add egg white to clarify.

- Dissolve gelatine over hot water.

- Strain stock and stir in gelatine. Add brandy and allow to cool. Place in a refrigerator.

- When aspic begins to thicken, spoon in a half inch layer into a well-oiled 9" mould. Arrange slices of egg and olives in a design. Spoon over another layer of aspic. Return to refrigerator to set.

- Mix ham cubes and sausage meat with remaining aspic.

- Remove mould from refrigerator. Arrange half the chicken slices, spoon over ham and sausage mixture, cover with remaining chicken, spoon over remaining aspic and return to refrigerator till set.

- To serve, turn out mould onto a serving dish and garnish with tomato wedges and sprigs of parsley.

Mutton & Beef

B eef in Goa is not of good quality. Usually old, useless cattle are slaughtered, and it requires all the ingenuity of Goan cooks to render it tender and palatable. Beef ranks third in preference, pork and chicken being the favourites, and the repertoire is somewhat limited. Most dishes were developed outside Goa but nevertheless have a distinct Goan flavour.

Mutton hardly figures in Goan cuisine. A small Goan Muslim community slaughters goats for their own consumption only. It is hardly ever sold in the market and the Goan Hindu rarely eats meat.

XACUTI DE CARNEIRO
Mutton Curry

Serves: 6-8

This dish holds pride of place in the Goan Hindu repertoire of recipes—indeed, even the Goan Christian admits that his Hindu brother makes a better xacuti.

1 kg mutton, cut into pieces for curry
20 dried red chillies, deseeded
1½" piece whole turmeric
15 cloves
3" piece cinnamon
2 tbsp cumin seeds
2 tbsp coriander seeds
6 peppercorns
2 tbsp aniseed (saunf)
1 tbsp caraway seeds (shahi jeera)

157

2 flakes mace (javitri)
6 medium onions
3 tbsp oil
1 large coconut, grated
5 green chillies
1 small bunch coriander leaves
10 cloves garlic
3" piece ginger
Salt to taste
Tamarind the size of a large walnut, soaked in 1 cup water
Fine slivers of coconut for garnish (optional)

- Dry roast red chillies, turmeric, cloves, cinnamon, cumin seeds, coriander seeds, peppercorns, aniseed, caraway seeds, and mace individually on a tava or griddle. Grind and keep aside.

- Slice one onion and chop remaining.

- Heat one tablespoon oil in a pan and fry sliced onion till opaque, add half grated coconut and fry till brown. Grind and keep aside.

- Grind together green chillies, coriander leaves, garlic and ginger. Mix into mutton and allow to marinate for 20 minutes.

- Heat 2 tablespoons oil in a pressure cooker and fry half chopped onions till brown. Add marinated mutton, remaining chopped onions and salt. Fry for 1-2 minutes. Add ground coconut and onion mixture. Mix well and add one cup water.

- Pressure-cook for 15 to 20 minutes after the first whistle. Let cooker cool before opening.

- Extract ¾ cup thick milk from remaining coconut.

Add to mutton with ground dry masala. Stir well.

- Squeeze out tamarind pulp and add to xacuti.

- Place cooker on heat and simmer till gravy thickens. Adjust seasoning.

- Garnish with fine slivers of fresh coconut and serve with rice or oddé.

PAO RECHEADO COM CARNE PICADA
Stuffed Mince Loaf

Serves: 6-8

Try out this recipe to glamorize the ordinary! It is perfect
served with a fresh green salad.

1 sandwich bread loaf
½ coconut, grated
2 tbsp oil
2 onions, finely sliced
6 cloves garlic, chopped
1" piece ginger, sliced
4 green chillies, sliced
¾ kg minced meat
½ tsp cumin powder
1 tbsp vinegar
Salt to taste
1 egg, beaten

Finely ground:

4 cloves
8 peppercorns
1" piece cinnamon

- Cut off top of loaf carefully, about ¼" thick and
  keep aside. Hollow out loaf, leaving a ¼" thick
  crust. Crumble half the soft part.

- Extract 2 cups milk from grated coconut.

- Heat oil in a pan and fry onions, garlic, ginger and
  chillies, till onions turn brown. Add mince and fry
  thoroughly. Add cumin powder and ground spices.

- Add vinegar and salt and cook till mince is done, adding a little hot water if required. The mixture should be a little moist. Remove from heat and cool.

- Spoon just enough coconut milk carefully along lid, sides and base of loaf case to moisten. The case should not sag with moisture.

- Add egg to mince and just enough crumbled soft bread to fill loaf.

- Adjust seasoning and fill mince into loaf case. Cover with lid, and bake in preheated oven at 200°C (400°F) for about 30 minutes, till browned.

- Place loaf on a platter and serve with a fresh green salad.

CARNE PICANTE COM BATATA-DOCE
Savoury Mince with Sweet Potatoes

Serves: 4

The sweet potatoes contrast well and serve as a foil to the piquant mince.

¾ kg ground meat
1 tbsp oil
2 medium onions, chopped
½ tsp turmeric powder
1½ tbsp recheio masala
Salt to taste
½ cup water
4 sweet potatoes, boiled and cubed
Chopped coriander leaves for garnish

- Heat oil in a pan and fry onions till brown. Add turmeric powder and cook for one minute.

- Add ground meat and stir to mix. Stir in masala, salt and water.

- Cook meat over medium heat till done. It should be moist and not too dry. Adjust seasoning.

- Arrange mince down centre of serving dish with potatoes on either side.

- Garnish with chopped coriander leaves and serve.

CASSEROLE DE CARNE
Baked Savoury Mince with Potatoes

Serves: 6-8

This is not a true casserole but actually a 'bake', and a good way to cheer up the last of the roast beef.

½ kg roast beef
2 Goa sausages, cooked and skins removed
6 large potatoes
2 tbsp butter
1½ cup milk
Salt and pepper to taste
6 large tomatoes, sliced
1 large egg

- Cut meat into pieces and mince together with sausages.

- Boil potatoes and mash, adding butter and milk. Season with salt and pepper.

- Butter a pie-dish and spread half the potato over base. Cover with half the tomatoes. Spoon in mince and spread over tomatoes. Cover mince with remaining tomatoes, and then remaining potato.

- Beat egg and brush top. Bake in a preheated oven at 175°C (350°F) for about 30-45 minutes, till brown.

BOLINHAS DE CARNE EM CARIL VERDE
Meatballs in Green Curry

Serves: 6

A change from red curries! The mince must be finely ground, not merely minced.

Meatballs:

½ cup finely ground mince
2 slices bread with crusts removed, crumbled
1 tsp cumin powder
Salt to taste

Curry:

1 tbsp oil
1 medium onion, chopped
½ tsp cumin powder
½ tsp coriander powder
3-4 tbsp chopped fresh coriander leaves
Pulp from tamarind the size of a walnut soaked in ½ cup water
Salt to taste

Ground to a smooth paste:

½ medium fresh coconut
6 cloves garlic
1" piece ginger
6 medium green chillies

Finely ground:

6 peppercorns
1" piece cinnamon
Seeds of 4 green cardamoms

Meatballs:

- Mix all ingredients together till well blended.

- Let mixture rest for one hour.

- Oil palms of hands and shape into balls the size of large marbles, pressing each meatball firmly.

- Keep aside.

Curry:

- Heat oil in a pan and fry onion till opaque. Stir in ground coconut paste, cumin and coriander powders. Add one tablespoon water and fry for 2 minutes, stirring to prevent mixture sticking.

- Stir in ground dry spices, 1½ cups water, coriander leaves and tamarind pulp. Stir to mix. Add salt to taste.

- Simmer for about 30 minutes. Add more water if necessary to keep quantity stable. Adjust seasoning.

- Turn up heat and gently slide in meatballs. Simmer for 5 minutes, remove from heat and serve.

CARIL DE BIFE
Curried Beef

Serves: 6-8

A mildly spiced dish, it is best served with wheat flour chapatti.

1 kg beef cut in cubes
Salt to taste
2 tbsp oil
3 onions, sliced
Pulp from tamarind the size of a large walnut soaked in ½ cup water
½ tsp sugar (optional)

Finely ground:

8 cloves garlic
1 tsp turmeric powder
1 tsp cumin seeds
1 tsp coriander seeds
1" piece cinnamon
8 peppercorns
1" piece ginger
6 cloves
6 green chillies

- Wash beef well, drain, apply salt and set aside.

- Heat oil in a pan and fry onions till brown. Add ground spices and fry well.

- Add meat and mix thoroughly. Reduce heat and simmer adding a little hot water as required.

- When half done, add tamarind pulp and sugar if

desired.

- Adjust seasoning. The gravy should be thick. It should take about 1½ hours for the meat to be done.

- Serve with fried sliced potatoes and wheat flour chapatti.

Note: Cooking time would be reduced to 45 minutes in a pressure cooker.

BIFE À PAIS DE GOA
Goa Country-style Beef

Serves: 6-8

This simple recipe was ideal for the often tough meat available in Goa. It was usually cooked in a kundlem, a shallow mud vessel, and it took all day to get ready, simmering quietly on the chulha.

Today, one can hurry the process with a pressure cooker, but the flavour is not quite the same.

1 kg beef
1 small pod garlic
1½" piece ginger
4 green chillies, deseeded
1" piece whole turmeric
Juice of 2 limes
Salt to taste
1 tbsp vinegar
4 potatoes, boiled
2 tbsp oil
4 medium onions

- Cut meat into slices and beat with a mallet to tenderize.

- Grind garlic, ginger, chillies and turmeric together. Mix with lime juice, salt and vinegar and apply to meat. Allow to marinate for 2 hours.

- Peel and slice potatoes. Heat oil in a pan and fry potatoes. Remove with a slotted spoon.

- Add onions and fry lightly. Add meat with marinade

and 2 cups water. Bring to boil then simmer for about ¾-1 hour, till done. Adjust seasoning.

- Serve garnished with fried potato slices.

BIFE BAFAD
Thick Beef Curry

Serves: 6

The radish lends a special flavour to the dish, which may be served with a fugad of French beans and chapatti.

1 kg beef, cut in cubes
2 tbsp oil
3 medium onions, chopped
1½" piece ginger, ground
8 cloves garlic, ground
2 medium tomatoes, chopped
1½ tbsp bafad masala
1 tbsp vinegar
Salt to taste
3 white radish, cut in fingers

- Heat oil in a pan and fry onions, ginger and garlic till golden brown. Add tomatoes and stir in masala. Fry for 2 minutes, adding a little water if necessary to prevent sticking.

- Add meat and mix well with masala. Add vinegar, salt and 2 cups water. Bring to boil, put in radish, and simmer for about 1½ hours, till done, adding a little water if necessary.

- It should take about 45 minutes in a pressure cooker.

- The gravy should be thick.

BIFE COM CEBOLAS
Onion Steaks

Serves: 6-8

1 kg undercut or filet of beef
10 peppercorns, ground
8-10 cloves garlic, ground
Salt to taste
1 tsp raw papaya, ground
1 tbsp vinegar
3 tbsp oil
4 potatoes, boiled and sliced
3 medium onions, cut in rings
1 tbsp refined flour (maida)
1 tbsp Worcestershire sauce
½ cup water

- Wash filet and pat dry. Cut into ½" thick slices.

- Mix ground peppercorns, garlic, salt, papaya and vinegar. Rub into meat slices and marinate for 1-2 hours.

- Heat one tablespoon oil in a heavy skillet or frying pan. Fry potatoes till golden-brown and keep aside.

- Add more oil to pan, fry onions till brown and keep aside.

- Add remaining oil and fry steaks a few at a time, for 3 minutes on each side and remove to a serving dish.

- Lower heat and stir flour into skillet, adding a little more oil if necessary. Cook for 2 minutes.

- Stir in water and Worcestershire sauce and cook to

make a thick gravy. Adjust seasoning.

- Pour sauce over steaks, arrange onions and potatoes on top and serve hot.

ASSADO DE BIFE
Roast Beef

Serves: 6-8

1½ kg round of beef
8 cloves garlic
1" piece ginger
10 peppercorns
1 tsp turmeric powder
1 tsp cumin powder
Salt to taste
2 tbsp oil
3 cups hot water
1 tbsp vinegar
4 dried red Kashmiri chillies
6 cloves
2" piece cinnamon

- Wash meat well and pat dry. Prick meat thoroughly all over. Grind garlic, ginger and peppercorns. Rub well into meat with turmeric, cumin and salt. Marinate for one hour.

- Heat oil in large, heavy bottomed pan and brown meat on all slides. Add hot water, vinegar and remaining spices. Reduce heat, cover and simmer for about 2 hours, till meat is done and almost dry. Add more hot water if required.

Note: A pressure cooker would cut down cooking time dramatically, in which case just 1½ cup hot water would suffice. It should take about one hour to be done.

C

173

BIFE ENROLADO
Rolled Beef

Serves: 8-10

Spicy sausage meat makes this a special dish. It graces a party table well when garnished with boiled French beans, carrots and cauliflower florets.

Beef roll:

2 kg undercut of beef
Salt to taste
1 tbsp raw papaya paste (if beef is tough)
3-4 Goa sausages
3 onions, quartered
Oil for basting

Gravy:

½ tsp fat or oil
¾ tbsp refined flour (maida)
Salt to taste

Garnish:
Boiled cauliflower florets and diced French beans and carrots

Beef roll:

- Wash meat and pat dry. With a sharp knife, trim off all fat and tendons. Make cuts in meat to open and make it flat. Trim to shape into an oblong. Apply salt. If beef is tough rub with one tablespoon raw papaya paste. Set aside.

- Remove casing from sausages. Cook sausage meat

with onions and water for 10-15 minutes till fairly dry and done. Spread evenly on undercut. Carefully roll meat, starting at the narrower end. Tie securely with string.

- Coat undercut with oil and place in an oiled baking dish. Bake in a preheated oven at 175°C (350°F), basting with extra oil and turning undercut to brown all over. Cook for about one hour.

- Remove from oven and allow to cool.

Gravy:

- Add one cup hot water into baking pan and stir to mix drippings in pan.

- Heat oil in a saucepan, add flour and cook for one minute. Add liquid from roasting pan. Adjust seasoning.

To Serve:

- Untie string from roll, slice and arrange on platter. Pour on gravy and garnish with boiled vegetables.

ENROLADOS DE BIFE
Beef Rolls

Serves: 4

For some inexplicable reason, this is also known as 'beef olives'. This was one way of rendering the tough Goa beef palatable.

½ kg beef, cut into thick slices
5 cloves garlic, ground
½ tsp pepper, ground
Salt to taste
1 medium white radish, scraped and cut into fingers
2 tbsp oil
1 large onion, chopped
1 large tomato, chopped
2" piece cinnamon, broken in pieces
4 cloves
2 dried red chillies, deseeded
1 tbsp vinegar

- Beat beef slices into flat rectangles and trim off uneven edges. Mix garlic, pepper and salt and apply a little to each slice.

- Place a stick of radish on each slice and roll to form a sausage. Tie with string.

- Heat oil in a pan and fry rolls till well browned. Lift out and set aside.

- Add onions to pan and fry till brown. Add tomato and fry well, adding a little water if required.

- Add spices and chillies, stir and add rolls. Coat rolls well with mixture. Pour in vinegar and one cup water. Lower heat and cook for about ¾ hour, till done. Adjust seasoning.

- Serve with finger potato chips.

GUIZADO DE LINGUA A TIA ANU
Stewed Tongue a la Tia Anu

Serves: 6-8

Anunciacao, affectionately shortened to Anu was really a well-loved aunt. An excellent cook, there was always something utterly delicious cooked and ready for a visitor. Pressure cooking the tongue cuts down cooking time.

1 kg beef tongue
Salt to taste
1 tbsp oil
3 medium onions, sliced
3 green chillies, deseeded and slit
1 tbsp Worcestershire sauce
1½ cup water

Ground to a smooth paste:

1½" piece ginger
10 cloves garlic

Finely ground:

1" piece cinnamon
6 cloves
8 peppercorns

- Wash tongue well. Put enough water in a large pan to cover tongue. Bring water to boil, plunge in tongue and bring to boil again. Cook for 5 minutes. Remove tongue and peel off outer skin.

- Cut tongue into ¼" slices. Apply a little salt on sliced tongue.

- Heat oil in pressure cooker and fry onions till brown. Stir in ginger, garlic and ground dry spices and fry for 2 minutes adding a little water to prevent sticking.

- Add sliced tongue and fry well. Stir in green chillies, Worcestershire sauce, and water.

- Cook in pressure cooker for about one hour.

- Adjust seasoning and serve.

LINGUA ASSADA EM POTE
Pot-Roasted Tongue

Serves: 4-6

Sliced thin for sandwiches, or served on bread or toast as a snack, this makes a good stand-by for the busy housewife.

1-1½ kg beef tongue
8-10 cloves garlic, ground
8-10 peppercorns, ground
1 tsp salt
1 tbsp oil
1 tbsp vinegar
1½ cup water

Finely ground:

3 dried red chillies, deseeded
1½" piece cinnamon
4-6 cloves

- Wash tongue well. Put enough water in a large pan to cover tongue. Bring water to boil, plunge in tongue and bring to boil again. Cook for 5 minutes.

- Remove tongue and peel off outer skin.

- Prick tongue well all over with fork. Rub with ground garlic, pepper and salt. Marinate for one hour.

- Heat oil in a pressure cooker, add tongue and brown all over. Add remaining ingredients. Cook for about one hour.

- Lift out tongue.
- Reduce liquid to ½ cup. Adjust seasoning.
- Slice tongue, pour over liquid and serve.

ISCAS
Stir Fried Liver

Serves: 4-6

As children, we thought that grand-aunt Tia Rubertina, who had a decided Portuguese accent, could not pronounce 'whiskers', and so we accepted the long thin strands of liver as the whiskers of a tiger!

¾ kg liver
8 cloves garlic, ground
½ tsp peppercorn, coarsely ground
½ cup milk
1 tsp salt
4 large potatoes
Oil for deep frying potatoes
2 tbsp oil
2 tbsp white wine
½ tsp nutmeg powder

- Clean liver of all tendons and veins, wash well and cut into 1/8" thick sticks.

- Mix garlic, pepper, milk and salt. Mix with liver and allow to marinate for one hour.

- Peel and cut potatoes into thin sticks, rinse and toss with a little salt. Heat oil for frying in deep frying pan and fry potatoes. Drain and keep aside.

- Heat 2 tablespoons oil in a large pan, add liver and stir-fry for just 3-4 minutes. Liver must not be over cooked or it will be tough.

- Add wine and let it evaporate. Sprinkle in nutmeg powder, adjust seasoning, stir and remove from heat.

- Serve liver in a flat dish surrounded with potato sticks.

FIGADO COM CEBOLAS
Liver with Onions

Serves: 4

The liver must not be overcooked or it will be tough and leathery.

½ kg liver
6-8 cloves garlic, ground
8 peppercorns, powdered
1 tsp salt
2-3 tbsp oil
2 medium onions, sliced into rounds
2 large tomatoes, sliced into rounds
2 tbsp water
1 tbsp Worcestershire sauce
2 dry red chillies, deseeded

- Wash liver well. Peel off membrane. Cut into thin slices, trimming off any remaining membrane. Mix garlic, peppercorns and salt and apply to liver. Marinate for 30 minutes.

- Heat oil in large frying pan and fry onions till golden brown. Remove and keep aside.

- Fry tomato slices for about 2 minutes on each side. Remove and keep aside.

- Add a little more oil if required and fry liver for about one minute on each side. Remove and keep aside.

- Add water into frying pan, stir to loosen and

dissolve any particles adhering to pan. Add Worcestershire sauce and chillies. Add more water if necessary and simmer for 3 minutes to make a thin gravy. Adjust seasoning. Remove chillies.

- Arrange liver on serving dish and pour over gravy. Arrange onion rings and tomatoes on top.

- Serve with finger potatoes and green peas.

ALMONDEGAS DE MIOLO
Brain Cutlets

Serves: 4

2 sets brain
Salt to taste
1 egg, beaten
Breadcrumbs for coating
Oil for shallow frying

Finely ground:

1" piece ginger
6 cloves garlic
2 green chillies

- Wash brains thoroughly, remove any slivers of bone attached.

- Scald brains in boiling water. Cool and carefully remove membranes. With a sharp knife cut into ⅓" thick slices.

- Apply ground masala and salt to both sides of each slice. Dip in egg and coat with breadcrumbs.

- Shallow fry over medium heat for about 2 minutes on each side.

- Serve with slices of lime.

Pork

In Goa, no feast or celebration is complete without at least one preparation of pork. Pork ranks next to fish in popularity, perhaps because beef and mutton had to be brought in from neighbouring areas and so were more expensive. Also, pigs could be bred and reared in the backyard and slaughtered whenever the need arose. In villages, neighbours bought pork from each other and perhaps it was available more easily than beef. Before people became so conscious of cholesterol and calories, every respectable household in Goa had roast or curried pork in the larder besides garlands of sausages, so that the lady of the house was never caught unprepared. Long before any special event a porker is selected and carefully fed to yield the correct proportion of meat to fat. Every part is used, the blood—black sausage—is used in sorpotel, the spare ribs and bones cooked in aad maas and even the tripe is rendered deliciously tender in a spicy sauce. The fat is boiled down to lard and used to make the semolina pastry for pies.

The European tradition of using the blood of the slaughtered animal cooked with vinegar and made into blüdwurst or black sausage, was introduced to Goa cuisine by the Portuguese. Indeed, several Portuguese sausages have blood added to the ingredients.

LEITÃO ASSADO
Roast Suckling

Serves: 12-14

Usually given pride of place at the buffet table, a 'must' for weddings and celebrations, the pigling roasted to a golden brown, gladdened hearts and lifted spirits.

1 pigling, about 3-4 kg
½ tbsp cumin powder
Juice of 4 limes
3 tbsp vinegar
2 tbsp salt
Oil for basting

Ground to a smooth paste:

3 pods garlic
4" piece ginger
6 green chillies

Finely ground:

10 peppercorns
10 cloves
4" piece cinnamon

Stuffing:

2 tbsp oil
1 medium onion, chopped
1" piece ginger, chopped
6 cloves garlic, chopped
4 green chillies, deseeded and chopped
Liver and kidneys of pigling, finely chopped
10 peppercorns
2 bay leaves

Salt to taste
2-3 cups fresh breadcrumbs
1 egg, beaten

- Wash pigling and pat dry with kitchen towels.

- Mix together cumin powder, both sets of, ground spices, lime juice, vinegar and salt. Rub inside of pigling thoroughly with mixture and marinate for 1½-2 hours.

Stuffing:

- Heat oil in a pan and fry onions till golden brown. Add ginger, garlic and chillies and fry for one minute.

- Stir in chopped liver and kidneys, peppercorns and bay leaves, and cook till done. Add a little water if necessary.

- Add salt. Remove from heat and cool.

- Mix in breadcrumbs and egg. Adjust seasoning.

To Roast pigling:

- Drain off and reserve any juices and marinade from pigling. Fill with stuffing and sew up the opening.

- Place pigling on roasting tray with front legs straight ahead and back legs stretched straight back. Support head with an oven-proof cup or tumbler. Brush over with oil. Add reserved juices and marinade to tray.

- Roast in a pre-heated oven at 190°C (375° F) till

golden brown. Baste from time to time with juices. Cooking time will be about 2 hours.

- Serve with sliced tomatoes and lettuce.

Pork

ASSADO DE PORCO
Pot Roast of Pork

Serves: 10-12

Roast pork makes several appearances at the table. First perhaps at Sunday lunch, next fried in slices for dinner, then sandwiched in small bread loaves and finally as a chilli fry!

1 leg of pork, about 3 kg
1¼ tsp turmeric powder
2 tsp salt
2 tbsp oil
3 medium onions, chopped
4 red chillies, deseeded
3" piece cinnamon, broken into pieces
8 cloves
10 peppercorns
2 cups hot water
1 tbsp vinegar
1 tbsp feni (optional)

Finely ground:

1½" piece ginger
12 cloves garlic

- Wash pork well and pat dry with kitchen towels.

- Mix ground ginger and garlic, turmeric powder and salt and rub well over meat. Marinate for 12-24 hours.

- Heat oil in a large pan and brown meat, carefully

turning it over to brown all sides.

- Add onions, chillies and whole spices and pour over hot water, vinegar and feni.

- Bring to boil, then simmer for ¾ hour. Check level of water, adding more hot water to prevent meat from sticking. Simmer till meat is done.

- Lift meat onto a serving dish. Add enough hot water to pan to make one cup gravy, stir to dissolve deposit. Adjust seasoning. Pour over meat and serve.

PERNAS DE LEITÃO ASSADO
Roast Suckling Hams

Serves: 4-6

The suckling piglets should not be longer than sixteen inches from snout to tail. Older piglings will prove to be tough. The cooked meat should be tender enough to cut with a fork.

> 4 rear legs—shanks and thighs of suckling piglets
> ½ tbsp salt
> 2 tbsp vinegar
> 3 tbsp oil or lard
> Lime wedges for garnish

Finely ground:

> 3 tsp turmeric powder
> 1½ tsp cumin seeds
> 15 cloves
> 2" piece cinnamon
> 1 tsp peppercorn

Ground to a smooth paste:

> 4" piece ginger
> 1 pod garlic

- Wash hams thoroughly. Rub well with powdered spices, salt, ginger and garlic. Prick all over with a skewer or long-tined fork. Pour over vinegar, making sure all surfaces are wet. Allow to marinate for 2 hours.

- Heat oil or lard in a large, heavy pan. Place hams so as not to overlap. Brown on one side, then on the other. Cover with a lid to fit inside pan and place a weight on top. Cook over low heat for 15-20 minutes.

- Remove hams to serving dish.

- Add ½ cup boiling water to pan and dissolve any masala and juice left. Pour over hams and serve garnished with wedges of lime.

VINDALHO DE PORCO
Spicy Pork Curry

Serves: 6-8

Vindaloo, as this dish is commonly known, is almost a pickle—no water is used and the slow cooking ensures that the spices penetrate through the meat. This dish keeps so well that it used to be carried on long journeys.

1 kg pork, belly portion, cut into 2" cubes
2 medium onions, finely chopped
1½ tsp salt
½ tsp sugar
1 tsp cumin powder
1 tsp turmeric powder
1 tsp chilli powder
Vinegar, as required
8 cloves
10 peppercorns
3" piece cinnamon, broken into pieces

Finely ground:
1 pod garlic
1½" piece ginger

- Wash meat and pat dry.

- Mix ground ginger, garlic, onion, salt, sugar and spice powders with about 4 tablespoons vinegar. Marinate meat in this mixture for least 12 hours.

- Put meat in a pan, cover and set on low heat. Cook till juices exude, stir occasionally to prevent meat from sticking.

- Continue cooking, adding a tablespoon of vinegar at a time, as required, stirring occasionally.

- When meat is half-done, add whole spices and cook for ¾-1 hour till tender. Adjust seasoning.

- Serve hot with bread or oddé.

SARAPATEL
Spicy Curry of Pork and Liver

Serves: 10-12

Best known of Goan pork dishes, it is called Sorpotel in Konkani. Every cook claims his own recipe to be the finest! It improves with age, and should be cooked 3-4 days ahead, and heated once a day to help it mellow. It is a versatile dish and may be served with a pulau, bread, Sana or oddé; and on toast it makes an irresistible snack! As for vinegar, my brother-in-law Lenny declared, 'You can never put too much vinegar into Sorpotel.'

1½ kg pork
½ kg liver
2 tbsp oil
2 onions, sliced
Vinegar to taste
Salt to taste
2 tbsp feni (optional)
Dried red Goa chillies or chilli powder to taste (optional)

Finely ground:

6 tsp turmeric powder
4" piece cinnamon
1 pod garlic
1 tsp cumin seeds
12 peppercorns
12 cloves
Seeds of 6 green cardamoms
15 dried red Kashmiri chillies

• Cut meat and liver into large pieces. Boil each

separately in just enough water to cover for 30 minutes. Reserve liquids. Cut meat and liver into small cubes.

- Heat oil in a pan and fry onions till brown. Add ground spices and fry well. Add to reserved liquids.

- Add meat to pan, fatty pieces first and fry on low heat. Add lean pieces of meat and then liver. Fry well and add to reserved liquids.

- Simmer meat on very low heat for at least 2 hours. The secret is the slow cooking, so be patient! Add vinegar, salt and feni, if using. Cool and leave aside for 24 hours. Keep it in a refrigerator if the weather is hot.

- Next day, heat through on low heat. Adjust seasoning. Add dried red chillies or chilli powder for pungency if desired.

- Repeat process for two days more. The meats should 'belong' to the gravy by now. The feni added with vinegar helps a lot.

CABIDELA
Curried Pigling

Serves: 6-8

1 kg pigling, including heart, liver and kidneys
2 tbsp oil or lard
3 medium onions, finely sliced
1 tsp cumin powder
2 tsp chilli powder
1½ tsp turmeric powder
Salt to taste
1 tbsp tamarind pulp
2 green chillies, slit (optional)

Ground to a smooth paste:
2" piece ginger
1½ pods garlic

Finely ground:
8 cloves
10 peppercorns
4" piece cinnamon

- Wash meat, heart, liver and kidneys, cut into one inch pieces and salt lightly.

- Heat oil in a pan and fry onions till brown. Add all the meat and fry well. Stir in ginger and garlic paste and cook over medium heat till juices begin to exude.

- Sprinkle in cumin, chilli and turmeric powders along with ground dry spices and salt. Stir well. Add a little hot water if necessary and cook on medium heat till meat is almost done, about 30 minutes.

- Add tamarind pulp and green chillies if desired. Cook for about 10-15 minutes more.

- Adjust seasoning and serve.

Pork

AADMAAS
Meat Bone Curry

Serves: 4-6

Spareribs and bones left over after removing the meat for sausages are cooked in this soul food. It eases the long wait before the sausages themselves are ready to eat. Of course, the bones have a little meat left on them by a sympathetic cook!

1 kg bones, washed well and cut into pieces
1½ tbsp oil
3 medium onions, chopped
2 tbsp recheio masala
2 cups hot water
1 tsp sugar
4 green chillies, slit
Salt to taste
1 tbsp tamarind pulp

- Heat oil in a pan and fry onions till opaque. Add recheio masala and fry for one minute.

- Add bones and stir to coat with mixture. Add hot water, sugar and chillies. Stir in salt.

- Cook covered, over medium heat, for ¾-1 hour till meat begins to leave bones. Stir in tamarind pulp, and enough hot water for sufficient gravy. Adjust seasoning.

- Serve with chapatti.

PEET-ACHEM MAAS
Savoury Pork Stew

Serves: 12

In a lightly spiced stew, vinegar and tamarind balance the richness of the pork. This stew is best eaten with wheat flour chapatti.

1½ kg pork, cut in 1" cubes marinated with 1 tsp turmeric powder
and 2 tbsp vinegar for 2 hours
Tamarind the size of a large walnut, soaked in 4 cups water
2 tbsp finely chopped fresh coriander
4 green chillies, finely sliced
2 tbsp oil
2 large onions, sliced
¼ kg (3 large) tomatoes, sliced
Salt to taste
¼ cup vinegar

Ground to a smooth paste:
½ pod garlic
3" piece ginger

Finely ground:
6 cloves
3 tsp turmeric powder
10 peppercorns
Seeds of 6 green cardamoms
1 tsp cumin seeds
3" piece cinnamon

- Extract tamarind pulp and add extra water to make 4 cups. Add fresh coriander and green chillies.

- Heat oil in a pan. Add fatty pieces of meat and fry for a few minutes. Add remaining meat and fry for a further few minutes, till brown. Remove meat with a slotted spoon and add to tamarind water.

- Add onions to pan and fry in residue fat till soft. Add ginger and garlic paste, fry for a minute and add tomatoes. Cook for a few minutes more. Add to meat.

- Add ground dry masala to meat and cook on low heat for 45 minutes, till tender.

- Add salt, vinegar and a few more chillies, if desired.

- Heat through and serve with whole wheat chapatti.

CARNE DE PORCO EM 'MARINADA BRANCA'
Pork with Feni

Serves: 6-8

Feni gives this Iberian recipe a Goan flavour. Black pepper and red chillies provide a good contrast to the pale gold of the meat.

1 kg shoulder or leg of pork
1½ tsp salt
½ cup vinegar
½ cup feni
2-3 large dried red Goa chillies, deseeded
8-10 peppercorns

Finely ground:

12 peppercorns
12 cloves garlic

- Debone meat and remove skin. Cut into 3 large pieces. Apply garlic and pepper to meat with salt. Place meat in a china or glass dish, add vinegar and feni. Marinate for 2-3 days, turning the pieces twice a day. Keep in a cool place, preferably in the refrigerator.

- Transfer meat to a pan, pour on marinade and one cup water. Place pan on heat and cook, turning occasionally. When nearly done, add chillies and whole peppercorns. There should not be too much liquid. Adjust seasoning and cook till tender. It should take about one hour.

- To serve, carefully lift out meat pieces, slice thickly and arrange in flat dish. Pour on liquid and arrange chillies as a garnish.

TAMREAL DE PORCO
Pork Stew

Serves: 6-8

Unsophisticated and simple to make, this is definitely soul food to be enjoyed with sana.

1 kg pork, belly portion, cut in cubes and salted
1 tsp cumin powder
1 tsp turmeric powder
½ tbsp chilli powder
12 cloves garlic, ground
2" piece ginger, ground
8 onions, sliced
5 green chillies, slit
¾ cup vinegar

Finely ground:

2" piece cinnamon
10 cloves
Seeds of 4 green cardamoms

- Mix all ingredients and cook on a low heat till done.
- Serve with sana.

PORCO COM CASTANHAS DE JACA
Pork with Jackfruit Seeds

Serves: 4-6

Because pork is a rich meat, there is no oil used in this recipe. The jackfruit seeds attain the texture of potatoes, but have a special delicate flavour of their own.

½ kg pork, belly cut
Salt to taste
½ tsp cumin powder
½ tsp pepper powder
6 cloves garlic
4 green chillies, chopped
1" piece ginger
2 dried red chillies, broken into pieces
2 onions, chopped
4 pieces dried kokum
20 jackfruit seeds

- Wash and cut pork into one inch pieces, apply salt and set aside for half an hour.

- Put pork in a pan with water just enough to cover. Bring to boil. Reduce heat and simmer.

- Stir in next 6 ingredients and cook till pork is half done.

- Add onion, kokum and jackfruit seeds.

- Continue to cook on low heat till pork and jackfruit seeds are tender. Adjust seasoning and serve.

COSTELETAS DE PORCO EM FENI
Pork Chops in Feni

Serves: 4

8 pork chops
Salt to taste
1-1½ tbsp recheio masala
1½ tbsp feni
Oil or lard for shallow frying
3 medium onions, sliced into rounds
3 dried red chillies, deseeded and sliced
½ cup hot water

- Wash and trim chops, cut off excess fat and salt lightly.

- Rub recheio masala evenly on both sides of chops, sprinkle over with feni and marinate for one hour.

- Heat oil in a pan, fry onion rings till brown and drain on paper towel.

- Fry chops for about 5 minutes on each side and lift onto serving dish.

- Add hot water to pan and stir to dissolve any deposit. Add chillies and cook till chillies are limp. Adjust seasoning and pour over chops.

CARNE DE PORCO SALGADA
Salted Pork

In the days before refrigeration, salted pork was cooked and eaten within a week, but since it was usually only prepared for a special occasion, it rarely lasted that long.

Choose a fairly lean piece of pork.

> 3 kg lean pork, deboned and kept in 1 piece
> 6 cubes (600 gm) jaggery
> Juice of 6 limes
> Peel of 6 limes, cut into pieces

Finely ground:

> 3 tbsp cooking salt
> 2 tbsp salt petre
> 2" piece cinnamon
> 4 cloves

- Clean meat and remove any surplus fat. do not wash. Prick all over.

- Pour lime juice over meat and rub well. Rub in ground spice and salt mixture.

- Place meat in a large stainless steel or ceramic pan. Cover meat with lime peel. Put a small plate over meat and put a heavy weight on top. Tie a thick cloth over pan and keep in a cool place for one week.

- Once a day, rub marinade over meat, turn over and cover again.

- On the 9th or 10th day, wash meat well, roll tight and secure with a string.

- Place roll in a pan with 3 cups water and boil for 2-3 hours till done.

- Allow to cool in the liquid.

- Remove pork from liquid and remove string. Slice and serve.

PÉS DE PORCO TEMPERADOS
Trotters

Serves: 4-6

6 trotters, cleaned
3 green cardamoms
2" piece cinnamon
8 peppercorns
1 tbsp oil
2 onions, sliced
1 tbsp sugar
1 cup vinegar
Salt to taste

Finely ground:

1 tsp cumin powder
1½" piece ginger
1 tsp turmeric powder
8 peppercorns
Seeds of 4 green cardamoms
1 pod garlic
1½ tsp Kashmiri chilli powder

- Place trotters in pressure cooker with whole cardamoms, cinnamon and peppercorns. Add water to cover by 2 inches. Pressure cook for one hour.

- Heat oil in a pan and fry onions till brown. Add ground spices and cook till oil separates. Add to trotters.

- Simmer for 30 minutes. Add vinegar, sugar and salt. Stir and serve hot.

213

CHOURIÇO DE GOA
Goa Sausages

Makes: 15-18 sausages

Goa sausages, spicy and quick-cooking, are to this day a stand-by for the hostess taken by surprise. They were very tedious to make in the days before refrigeration when the meat had to be dried and stuffed into casings. However, today the meat filling can be stored in a glass jar in the refrigerator. It keeps for 2-3 months and the equivalent of one to two sausages can be spooned out and cooked in a jiffy. The flavour depends very much on the quality of vinegar used. This recipe produces a fairly mild version of the sausage.

1½ kg pork, skinned
1½ tbsp + 1 tsp salt
8 cloves
Seeds of 6 green cardamoms
1 tsp cumin seeds
8 peppercorns
1 pod garlic
20 dried red Kashmiri chillies
6 tsp turmeric powder
4" piece cinnamon
2 cups vinegar
2 metres guts

- Cut meat into ½" cubes. Wash, and drain. Mix in 1½ tablespoon salt, tie in a cloth and hang bundle to drip for 4 hours. The meat may be dried further in the sun for 10 hours.

- Grind all spices in vinegar. Place meat in glass or china jar. Add spices and one teaspoon salt and mix well. The mixture should be fairly moist. Add more vinegar if required. Tie thick, double cloth over mouth of jar and store in refrigerator.

- The mixture should be stirred once a week. It is ready for use after 2 weeks.

- Use only a clean, dry stainless steel spoon to mix or to remove sausage meat for cooking.

To make sausages:

- Thoroughly clean and wash guts in vinegar and dry. Cut into 2 lengths.

- Wash and dry a large mango leaf, cut off 2" from end, insert into one end of gut.

- Fill in sausage meat down the mango leaf with spoon and fingers, pushing it along the length of the gut.

- With strong string tie gut at 4" intervals, and at both ends.

- Dry sausages in the sun for 3-4 days then indoors in a dry well ventilated place. The sausages can be smoked over a wood fire.

- If sausages are to be stored for long, place in air-tight container and pour in enough oil to cover. Seal firmly.

Note: Guts are available at pork shops on order.

FEIJOADA
Goa Sausages with Dried Beans

Serves: 6-8

This recipe was carried by Portuguese caravels across the Atlantic to Brazil and around the Cape to Goa where it became a favourite. The Portuguese and Brazilian versions call for salt pork but in Goa spicy sausages add zest to the dish. Slow cooking is the secret. For a richer dish, the onions may be fried in a little oil.

1½ cup dried black eyed beans (chora) or kidney beans (rajma)
2 large onions, chopped
2 large tomatoes, skinned and chopped
2 large Goa sausages
Salt to taste

- Wash beans and soak in water overnight.

- Remove skin from sausages and break up meat.

- Put sausage meat into a large pan with beans, onions, tomatoes and water to cover by half an inch. Add salt to taste.

- Cook over low heat for about 30 minutes, stirring occasionally till beans are soft and gravy thickens. Adjust seasoning.

CHOURIÇO DO REINO
Portuguese Sausages

Makes: 45-50 sausages

'Sausages of the kingdom' is the literal translation. They are truly royal, delicate in flavour, and pale golden-brown in colour.

5 kg pork, without skin; bone and excess fat trimmed off
125 gm (½ cup) salt
3 tsp salt petre
3 tsp sugar
2 tsp, powdered bay leaves (tej patta)
1½ cups tomato paste, condensed
Juice of 2 limes
1 pod garlic, finely sliced
1 tsp powdered cloves
1 tsp coarsely ground pepper
1 cup dry white wine
½ cup feni
¾ cup olive oil

- Wash and wipe meat dry. Cut into small cubes, add salt and mix thoroughly.

- Tie in a clean cloth and hang in a cool place with a pan underneath to catch the drip. Leave overnight.

- Next day, put meat into a bowl with remaining ingredients and mix well.

- Place a plate inside pan with a weight on it. Tie a cloth over pan and keep in a cool place, for two days. Stir and mix meat once a day, replacing weight and cloth cover.

- Fill into prepared guts as given for Chouriço de Goa, tying a string every 6 inches or so.

- Hang on a rod and dry in a warm, airy spot, out of the direct sun, for two days. Smoke over a wood fire till they turn a pale brown.

Note: The guts are available at pork shops on order.

Vegetables

While the diet of the Goan Hindu lays emphasis on vegetarian dishes, the Goan Christian households often have an arrangement with a local fisherman to deliver a measure of prawns daily to the kitchen. Their vegetables are cooked as an accompaniment to a main dish of fish, meat or poultry. Most cooks love to toss in a few small prawns and a little grated coconut but this addition is optional.

TAMBADI BHAJI
Savoury Red Amaranthus

Serves: 4-6

Red amaranthus leaves are a favourite vegetable, specially cooked with grated coconut. The leaves should be freshly plucked as the flavour spoils if allowed to wilt.

1 large bunch red amaranthus leaves (tambadi or cholai bhaji)
1 onion
4 cloves garlic
2 green chillies, deseeded if desired
1 tbsp oil
1 tbsp grated coconut
Salt to taste

- Pick leaves off stalks, chop coarsely and wash well to remove any mud. Drain in a sieve.

- Slice onion, garlic and green chillies. Heat oil in a pan and fry till onions are soft.

- Add leaves, cover and cook over low heat. Stir

frequently to prevent sticking.

- When nearly done, stir in coconut and salt to taste.
- Serve immediately.

Note: 1 tbsp small prawns, cleaned and deveined can be added along with coconut. Cook till prawns curl up.

FUGAD DE REPOLHO
Savoury Cabbage with Coconut

Serves: 3-4

Easy to cook and good with either meat or fish.

¼ kg cabbage, finely sliced
1 tbsp oil
1 medium onion, finely sliced
½" piece ginger, sliced
2 cloves garlic, sliced
2 green chillies, deseeded and sliced
Salt to taste
1 tbsp grated coconut

- Heat oil in a pan and fry onion, ginger, garlic and green chillies till onions are soft.

- Stir in cabbage, add salt, cover and cook over low heat for 5 minutes. Add a spoonful of water if required.

- When done stir in coconut and serve immediately.

Variations:

- **Fugad de chitkeo mitkeo (Savoury cluster beans with coconut)**: Substitute ¼ kg cluster beans (gwar phali), trimmed and chopped in place of cabbage.

- **Fugad de feijão verde (Savoury French beans with coconut)**: Substitute ¼ kg trimmed, chopped French beans in place of cabbage.

- **Fugad de rabanete (Savoury white radish with**

coconut): Use ¼ kg white radish, cut into matchstick pieces, in place of cabbage. Add some of its tender leaves, chopped.

- **Fugad de xengo (Savoury drumsticks with coconut):** Use ¼ kg drumsticks, peeled and cut in 2" pieces or the tender leaves and flowers of the drumstick tree, in place of cabbage.

MERGOL DE QUIABOS
Okra—Goan Style

Serves: 3-4

A simple recipe that looks and tastes good and is a favourite with cholesterol watchers.

¼ kg okra (bhindi), cut in rings
2 green chillies, chopped
1 medium onion, chopped
3 cloves garlic, sliced
1 large tomato, chopped
¼ " piece ginger, sliced
1 tsp vinegar
Salt and sugar to taste

- Put all ingredients in a pan. Cover and cook over low heat, stirring to prevent sticking. Add a spoonful of water if required. Cook for about 10 minutes.

Variation:

- **Mergol de gosaim (Ridged gourd—Goan style):** Use ¼ kg ridged gourd (touri), peeled and cut into pieces and do not add vinegar.

- **Mergol de abóbora (Red pumpkin—Goan style):** Use ¼ kg red pumpkin, peeled and cubed and do not add vinegar.

SUQUEM DE ABÓBORA-I
Savoury Red pumpkin

Serves: 3-4

The sweetness of a well-ripened pumpkin is balanced by red chillies and ginger.

¼ kg red pumpkin (seetaphul or kuddu), skinned and cut into
1" cubes
1 tbsp oil
½ tsp cumin seeds
1 medium onion, sliced
4 cloves garlic, sliced
¼" piece ginger, sliced
¼ tsp turmeric powder
1 medium tomato, chopped
Salt to taste
2 large dried red chillies, sliced
Coriander leaves for garnish

- Heat oil in a pan, add cumin seeds and fry till they splutter. Add onion, garlic and ginger and fry till onions are soft.

- Add turmeric powder and fry for one minute.

- Add tomato and stir well. Put in pumpkin and salt, and mix.

- Add chillies. Cover and cook on low heat till done.

- Serve sprinkled with chopped coriander leaves.

SUQUEM DE ABÓBORA-II
Savoury Red Pumpkin

Serves: 3-4

¼ kg red pumpkin (seetaphul or kuddu), skinned and cut into
1" cubes
1 tbsp oil
1 medium onion, finely sliced
6 cloves garlic, finely sliced
½" piece ginger, finely sliced
1 medium tomato, chopped
¼ tsp coriander powder
2 green chillies, slit
Salt to taste
1 tbsp chopped fresh coriander

- Heat oil in a pan and fry onions, garlic and ginger till onions are opaque.

- Add tomato and fry for one minute. Sprinkle over coriander powder.

- Add pumpkin and green chillies. Stir to mix.

- Cover and cook over low heat for about 10 minutes. Add salt.

- Cover and cook for a further 3 minutes.

- Garnish with fresh coriander and serve.

Variation:

- **Abóbora com camarão** (Savoury red pumpkin with prawns): Sometimes, the cook cannot resist the urge of 'prawns with everything' and when the prawns are so fresh and flavoursome, who can blame him?

- Add 1 tbsp shelled small prawns, cleaned and deveined, with salt. Cook till prawns curl up.

CALDINHO DE ABÓBORA BRANCA
Mild Curry of White Pumpkin

Serves: 6-8

A caldinho is really a very mild, delicately flavoured curry and a versatile one.

Kohlrabi, sliced cabbage or even mixed vegetables—carrots, beans and green peas—taste good cooked this way.

½ kg white pumpkin (petha), cut into ⅓" slices
1 coconut, grated
½ tbsp coriander seeds
1 tsp cumin seeds
8 peppercorns
1" piece whole turmeric
6 cloves garlic
½" piece ginger
1 cup hot water
1 tbsp oil
1 medium onion, sliced
3 green chillies, slit
Salt to taste
Lime juice or vinegar to taste
1 tbsp chopped fresh coriander leaves

- Grind coconut with next 6 ingredients coarsely. Squeeze to extract thick milk.

- Add hot water to ground masala and extract thin milk.

- Heat oil in a pan and fry onion till opaque. Stir in thin coconut milk and add green chillies. Simmer over medium heat till onion turns limp.

- Put in sliced pumpkin and sprinkle with salt. Cook till pumpkin is done, about 10 minutes. Stir in thick coconut milk.

- Stir in lime juice or vinegar to taste.

- Add fresh coriander and serve.

Variation:

- **Caldinho de abóbora branca com camarão (Mild curry of white pumpkin with prawns)**: Add 2 tbsp prawns, cleaned and deveined with pumpkin.

PODOLLIM RECHEADO COM BATATA-DOCE
Snake Gourd Stuffed with Sweet Potatoes

Serves: 6

Be sure to choose tender gourds, there should be no fibres or else they will be tough when cooked.

2 snake gourds (chirchinda), about 18" long
3 cups savoury sweet potatoes (see recipe—Batata-doce picante)
Breadcrumbs as required
Butter or oil as required

- Wash gourds well and cut into 1½" sections. Clean out seeds.

- Fill each section of gourd with potato filling and place on end in an oiled baking dish.

- Sprinkle over with breadcrumbs and dot with butter or dribble over oil. Bake in a preheated oven at 190°C (375°F) for about 20 minutes.

Variation:

- **Podollim rechaeado com carne picada (Snake gourd stuffed with mince):** Use mince in place of potatoes. (See recipe—Pao recheado com carne picada)

- **Podollim recheado com camarão (Snake gourd stuffed with prawns):** Stuff snake gourd with savoury prawns. (See recipe—Camarão com cebolas)

SALADA DE REPOLHO
Cabbage Salad

Serves: 8-10

In Goa, cabbage is substituted for lettuce, which does not grow well in the humid climate. Because it keeps fresh longer than most other vegetables, the cabbage is widely used—cooked or in a salad. Combinations with carrots or kohlrabi make for variation. Goa vinegar and olive oil make a difference.

½ kg cabbage
1 medium onion
1 medium tomato
2 green chillies
1 tbsp vinegar
1½ tbsp oil
½ tsp sugar
1 clove garlic, crushed
Salt to taste
Pepper to taste

- With a sharp knife, cut out thick hard stalk of cabbage and shred leaves as finely as possible. Wash in cold salted water, drain and shake dry.

- Slice onions very fine, wash in salted water and separate layers. Shake off water.

- Wash tomato, cut in fine slivers.

- Wash, de-seed and shred chillies.

- Shake together vinegar, oil, sugar, garlic, salt and

pepper in a small jar.

- Mix all prepared vegetables in a bowl and pour dressing over.

- Chill before serving.

Note: Capsicum may be substituted for green chillies.

BATATA-DOCE PICANTE
Savoury Sweet Potatoes

Serves: 4

Serve with whole wheat phulka or puri for breakfast or tea, or crumble and mash and use as stuffing for aubergines or snake gourds.

½ kg sweet potatoes
1½ tbsp oil
1½ tsp mustard seeds
2 dry red chillies, broken into pieces
4 cloves garlic, ground
½" piece ginger, finely shredded
15-20 curry leaves
1 medium onion, chopped
Salt to taste
Lime juice to taste

- Boil, potatoes, peel and cut into rounds.

- Heat oil and fry mustard seeds over medium heat till they pop. Add next five ingredients in the order given, one after the other frying each for a few seconds before adding next. Cook till onions turn opaque.

- Stir in potatoes and mix well. Sprinkle with salt and lime juice and serve.

BERINGELAS FRITAS
Fried Sliced Aubergine

Serves: 4

1-2 aubergines, about 3" in diameter
1 tsp salt
6-8 tbsp gram flour (besan), sieved
½ tsp asafoetida (hing)
½ tsp turmeric powder
½ tbsp rice flour
½ tbsp coriander powder
1 tsp chilli powder
Salt to taste
Oil for shallow frying

- Wash aubergines, cut into ⅓" thick slices. Apply one teaspoon salt to sliced aubergine and keep aside for 30 minutes.

- Mix remaining ingredients, except oil with enough water to produce a coating batter.

- Heat oil in a frying pan, dip aubergine slices in batter and shallow fry over medium heat till golden brown.

- Drain on paper towel.

- This can be served as a tea-time snack.

SUQUEM DE BERINGELAS
Savoury Aubergines

Serves: 4

½ kg aubergines
1 tsp salt
1 tbsp oil
3 medium onions, sliced
1 tsp turmeric powder
2 medium tomatoes, chopped
2-3 tsp chilli powder
1 tsp cumin powder
1 tbsp tamarind pulp
1 tsp vinegar
1 tsp sugar
Salt to taste

Finely ground:

6-8 cloves garlic
1" piece ginger

- Wash and cut aubergines in cubes. Toss with one teaspoon salt and keep aside for about 30 minutes.

- Heat oil in a pan and fry onions over medium heat till opaque. Add ground garlic and ginger and turmeric powder. Fry for one minute.

- Stir in tomatoes. Add chilli powder and cumin powder. Fry for one minute more, adding a spoonful of water to prevent sticking.

- Stir in drained aubergine cubes and turn to coat with masala. Add tamarind pulp.

- Cover and cook over low heat, stirring occasionally to prevent sticking.

- Add vinegar, sugar, and salt to taste.

- Cook only till aubergines become soft but not mushy.

Note: Small aubergines with stalks left on and slit in 4 are also cooked this way. Slow cooking is the secret.

Variation:
Suquem de beringelas com camarão seco (Savoury aubergines with prawns): Wash and drain 1 tbsp small, fine, dried prawns and add to fried onions. Fry for one minute before adding tomatoes.
Beringelas recheadas (Stuffed aubergines): Aubergines may also be stuffed with a prawn mixture (See recipe—Camarão com cebolas) or a savoury mince (See recipe—Pao recheado com carne picada). They may then be baked or fried.

- Cut aubergines in half lengthwise and parboil in lightly salted water.

- Hollow out flesh, leaving ¼" thick layer. Mash flesh and mix with filling of choice.

- Stuff aubergines, top with breadcrumbs and shallow fry or bake in preheated oven at 190°C (375°F) for 15 minutes.

CARATINS PICANTES
Spicy Bitter Gourd

Serves: 2-4

The bitter gourd has several medicinal properties, and is especially beneficial for diabetics. The gourds are scraped, deseeded, sliced in rings, salted, left to stand for ½ -1 hour and rinsed. Dried crisp in the sun, a few 'chips' a day are said to help reduce the blood sugar level.

In some recipes, the bitterness may be largely reduced by parboiling or salting the cut vegetable and allowing it to stand for ½-1 hour. Surprisingly, the first bitter taste turns faintly sweet in the mouth. An interesting vegetable altogether!

¼ kg bitter gourd (karela)
1 tsp salt
1 tbsp oil
1 medium onion, chopped
½" piece ginger, ground
6 cloves garlic, ground
½ tsp turmeric powder
1½ tsp chilli powder
½ tsp cumin powder
1 tsp coriander powder
½ tbsp tamarind pulp
½ tsp sugar

- With a sharp knife, scrape off outer knobbly skin of bitter gourds. Cut into rounds and discard seeds. Apply salt and let it stand for 30 minutes.

- Rinse and squeeze out moisture. The vegetable may be parboiled at this stage, but be careful, not to overcook as it should remain firm.

- Heat oil in a pan and fry onion till opaque. Add ginger and garlic and fry lightly.

- Stir in spice powders, add a little water if required and fry for one minute.

- Add bitter gourds and stir to coat with masala, adding enough water to prevent mixture sticking to pan.

- Add tamarind pulp and sugar, adjust seasoning and cook over low heat, for about 5 minutes, stirring occasionally.

CARATINS RECHEADOS COM BATATA-DOCE
Bitter gourd Stuffed with Savoury Sweet Potatoes

Serves: 4-6

The prepared bitter gourds can also be stuffed with savoury mince or prawns—they taste good any style!

6 medium sized bitter gourds (karela)
Batter to coat, made with 2 tbsp flour, a pinch of salt and enough water to mix
2 cups savoury sweet potatoes (see recipe—Batata-doce picante)
Breadcrumbs for coating
Oil for deep frying

- With a sharp knife, scrape off outside knobby skin of bitter gourds.

- Make a long slit down one side of each and remove seeds.

- Rub salt inside and outside and let them stand for 30 minutes.

- Rinse bitter gourds and parboil till tender but firm. Lift out and cool.

- Fill each bitter gourd with potato mixture and press to close.

- Coat with batter, roll in breadcrumbs.

- Heat oil in a deep frying pan and deep fry bitter gourds till golden brown.

- Drain on paper towel and serve.

Variation:

- **Caratins recheados com camarão (Bitter gourd stuffed with prawns):** Use 2 cups savoury prawns (see recipe—Camarão com cebolas) in place of potatoes.

PREPARADO PICANTE DE JACA VERDE
Curried Tender Jackfruit

Serves: 6-8

A good jackfruit tree is usually hung with at least a dozen fruit at any given time. While the ripe fruit is good to eat, the tender raw fruit makes a delicious vegetable.

1 tender, raw jackfruit, about 1 kg
Salt to taste
1" piece whole turmeric
6 peppercorns
8 dried red chillies
1½ tbsp oil
1 tsp mustard seeds
4 cloves garlic, ground
1 medium coconut, grated
1 onion, sliced

- Apply a little oil to the hands. Cut off skin and chop pulp of jackfruit into small pieces. Boil in 3-4 cups water for about 30 minutes, till well-cooked. Add salt.

- Dry roast turmeric, peppercorn and chillies individually on a tava or griddle, taking care not to let the spices burn.

- Grind fine.

- Heat oil in a pan, add mustard seeds and fry till they pop. Stir in garlic and fry till brown. Add coconut, sliced onion and ground masala. Fry well. Add boiled jackfruit with water, simmer till sufficiently dry.

• Adjust seasoning and serve.

MELGOR
Black-eyed Beans with Coconut

Serves: 4-6

A stand-by during the fish-less monsoon days, melgor is delicious eaten with rice bakhri.

¼ kg black-eyed beans (lobia)
2 tsp chilli powder
¼ tsp cumin powder
½ tsp pepper powder
1 tbsp coriander powder
A large pinch turmeric powder
5 cloves garlic, ground
1" piece ginger, ground
½ coconut, finely ground
1½ tbsp oil
1 large onion, chopped
½ tbsp tamarind pulp
Salt to taste

- Wash beans and soak overnight.

- Put beans in a pan with water and boil till tender.

- Drain and set aside. Reserve water.

- Mix all powdered spices with ginger, garlic and coconut.

- Heat oil in a pan and fry onion till golden.

- Stir in spice mixture and ½ cup water. Cook over medium heat for 2-3 minutes.

- Add beans, tamarind pulp and salt. Pour in reserved

water in which beans were cooked and simmer for 10 minutes.

- Adjust seasoning and serve hot with rice bhakri.

SORAK
Curry Sauce

Serves: 4

This curry is usually made on days of fast, or when fish is not available, but it is too good to be an imposition.

2 cups milk extracted from 1 medium ground coconut
1 tbsp chilli powder
5 cloves garlic, ground
½ tsp cumin powder
½ tsp turmeric powder
1 medium onion, sliced
5 green chillies, slit
Pulp from tamarind the size of a walnut, soaked in ½ cup water
Salt to taste

- Place all ingredients in a pan, bring to boil, lower heat and simmer. Cook till onion is quite soft. Adjust seasoning and serve.

AGSAL
Pepper Water

Makes: 4 cups

Agsal is a type of pepper water, prepared as a digestive and eaten with boiled rice—it certainly settles the stomach, joggles the liver and no doubt clears the brain!

6 cloves garlic, ground
½ tsp cumin powder
½ tsp turmeric powder
6-8 dried red chillies, slit
½ tbsp oil
2 medium onion, finely sliced
8 pieces dried kokum
½ tsp sugar
Salt to taste

- Mix together garlic, cumin, turmeric and 6 cups water in a pan. Place pan on heat and bring to boil. Lower heat, add chillies and simmer for about 10 minutes.

- Heat oil in another pan and fry onions lightly. Add to pepper water with kokum, sugar and salt. Simmer till onions and kokum are limp and the agsal is reduced to 4 cups.

- Serve hot with boiled rice.

COCONUT KOKUM CURRY

Makes: 2 glasses

After a rich meal, the Goan Hindu usually served each
guest a few spoonfuls of this 'curry' as a digestive.

6 dried kokum
½ coconut, grated
2 green chillies
Salt to taste

- Soak kokum and salt in half a glass of water. Keep
  aside.

- Grind grated coconut with chillies and squeeze out
  thick milk.

- Mix coconut milk and kokum water. Add salt to
  taste.

- Serve cold.

Rice

R ice is the staple cereal in Goa and is eaten three to four times a day, in various guises.

At 11 am, it is served as 'kanji', soft cooked and eaten in its own liquid, with 'kal chi koddi' (yesterday's curry) cooked to an utterly delicious thick sauce.

Of course the mid-day meal has to be rice and fish curry. At tea time, the merenda or snack is usually made with rice, coconut and jaggery. In many households, rice and curry make for a very satisfying dinner!

If the repetition does not pall, it is because of the quality and flavour of the rice used.

Rice is usually cooked in a tallish vessel on a slow fire. A little salt is added when the rice is almost done.

ARROZ COM COCO
Coconut Rice

Serves: 4-6

Rather rich and delicious with either green meatball curry or chicken xacuti.

3 cups long grained rice
2 tbsp oil
2 medium onions, finely sliced
1" piece ginger, ground
6 cloves garlic, ground
½ tsp turmeric powder
2" piece cinnamon, broken into small pieces
6 cloves
4 green cardamoms
½ tsp peppercorn

2 cups milk extracted from 1 large ground coconut
Salt to taste

- Wash rice and drain well. Spread out on a towel to dry.

- Heat oil in a pan and fry onions till light brown in colour. Add ginger and garlic and fry for 2 minutes. Stir in turmeric powder and whole spices and mix well.

- Add rice and stir to mix thoroughly, making sure every grain is coloured with turmeric.

- Add enough water to coconut milk to make 6 cups. Pour into rice with salt to taste and stir.

- Close vessel with a tight lid, lower heat and cook for about 20-30 minutes, till rice is done.

ARROZ REFOGADO
Baked Rice Pulau

Serves: 8-10

'Baked rice' cooked with coals on the lid of the vessel over a wood fire—but a modern oven will do.

4 cups suroi or any fine rice (not basmati)
8 cups stock made from meat bones
½ tsp turmeric powder
5 onions, 4 sliced and 1 kept whole
1-2 Goa sausages
2 tbsp ghee (clarified butter)
2 tomatoes, sliced
12-14 cloves
Salt to taste
1 tbsp oil

Garnish:
Sliced hard-boiled eggs, optional
Sliced chepnim mangoes (See recipe Manganhas
salgado chepnim), optional

- Simmer stock with turmeric and one sliced onion. When onion is soft add sausages, being very careful not to break skin.

- Continue cooking for about 15 minutes more. Remove sausages very carefully and set aside.

- Strain stock. If desired, let it cool and remove any fat that forms.

- Wash rice and soak for a few minutes. Drain and

keep aside.

- Heat ghee in a pan and fry 2 sliced onions till golden. Add sliced tomatoes and rice. Mix well and fry till all liquid is absorbed.

- Add enough water to stock, to make 8 cups. Add to rice.

- Sink in a whole peeled onion studded on the surface with cloves. Add salt to taste.

- Cover and bake in a medium oven or cook over low heat, stirring once or twice with a fork.

- Test if rice is done and stock is absorbed.

- Heat oil in a pan and fry one sliced onion till brown.

- Spoon rice onto flat serving dish. Garnish with fried onion, meat from sausages and optional garnishes.

Note: Basmati rice should not be used in this dish as its flavour is too strong.

ARROZ DE CAMARÃO
Prawn Pulau

Serves: 8-10

This prawn pulau calls for small white prawns—none larger than medium sized prawns should be used. The prawn stock gives the dish an attractive prawn-pink colour.

500 gm shelled prawns, cleaned, deveined and salted (reserve shells)
3 medium onions, sliced
3 tomatoes, chopped
½ tsp turmeric powder
1 tsp coriander powder
2 bouillon cubes (optional)
4 cups long-grained rice
2 tbsp ghee (clarified butter) or oil
8 cloves garlic, sliced
½" piece ginger, sliced
½ tsp cumin powder
6 cloves
6 green cardamoms
1½" piece cinnamon, broken into pieces
4 green chillies, sliced and deseeded
Salt to taste
6-8 prawns with shells, boiled whole for garnish

- Put prawn shells in a large pan with 10 cups water, one onion, one tomato, turmeric and coriander powder. Bring to boil then simmer for 45 minutes. Strain and keep aside. This should give 8 cups of stock. Add bouillon cubes if using.

- Wash rice and drain thoroughly.

- Heat ghee or oil in a pan and fry remaining onions till golden. Stir in ginger, garlic and remaining tomatoes. Fry well and add cumin powder.

- Add prawns and fry only till they curl. Remove prawns from pan.

- Add cloves, whole cardamom and cinnamon to pan and stir. Add rice and stir to coat every grain. Put in fried prawns and mix well. Pour in 8 cups prawn stock, green chillies, and salt to taste. Cover and cook over low heat, till done. Stir once or twice with a long-tined fork.

- Serve garnished with whole boiled prawns.

ARROZ À PORTUGUESA
Pulau—Portuguese Style

Serves: 6-8

3 cups fine grained rice
Salt to taste
4 cloves
½ tsp peppercorn
3 tbsp butter
3 bananas
1 tbsp sultanas (kishmish)
1 tbsp cashew nuts

- Wash rice, drain and set aside for 10 minutes.

- Bring 6 cups water to boil in a pan. Add rice, salt, cloves and pepper. Lower heat and cook till all water is absorbed.

- Heat one tablespoon butter in another pan and lightly fry sultanas and cashew nuts. Drain and keep aside.

- Cut bananas in half, then slit lengthwise, add to pan and saute in butter.

- Remove spices from rice with a large fork. Add remaining butter and toss lightly to mix.

- Arrange rice on serving dish. Place bananas on top, scatter over with nuts and sultanas and serve.

Bondla

Breads

Leavened bread made with toddy—not yeast, is produced by the baker, while the housewife turns out deliciously light sana and oddé, both leavened with toddy.

SANA
Steamed Rice Cakes

Serves: 6-8

Light-as-feather steamed rice cakes with toddy to make them 'Goan'. For this, a special steamer is used, with small saucer shaped moulds, but a modern idli cooker, ramekins, or an egg poacher does very well.

The secret is in allowing the batter to rise to almost double its bulk— achieved only by using pure, fresh toddy.

½ kg (2½ cups) Goa parboiled rice
4 cups fresh toddy
1 large coconut
½ tsp salt
2 tbsp sugar

- Wash rice and soak overnight.

- Next morning, drain rice and grind fine using only toddy.

- Grate coconut and grind fine, using only toddy.

- Mix ground rice and coconut with salt and sugar. Mix thoroughly, adding enough toddy to make a thick batter.

- Cover vessel containing batter and leave in a warm

place to rise for about 3-4 hours, or till batter almost doubles in bulk.

- Pour into moulds and steam for about 15-20 minutes in a steamer, till firm.

- A skewer inserted should come out clean.

Breads

SANDON
Steamed Rice Cakes with Savoury or Sweet Filling

Serves: 6-8

Sana batter made with ½ kg Goa parboiled rice

Sweet filling 1:

> 1½ cup grated coconut
> ¾ cup grated jaggery
> A pinch of powdered cardamom seeds

- Mix all ingredients well.

Sweet filling 2:

> 20-25 pods of jackfruit of the 'rosao' variety
> Sugar to taste

- Grind jackfruit finely to a smooth pulp. Add sugar to taste.

Savoury filling 1:

> 1 tbsp oil
> 1 medium onion, sliced
> 1" piece ginger, chopped
> 4 cloves garlic, chopped
> 2 green chillies, chopped
> ½ tsp cumin powder
> ¼ kg minced meat
> 1 cup chopped cluster beans (guvad)
> 3 cloves, finely ground
> 8 peppercorns, finely ground
> ½" piece cinnamon, finely ground
> 1 tsp salt
> ½ tbsp vinegar

C

- Heat oil in a pan and fry onion till brown. Add ginger and garlic and fry for 2 minutes. Add chillies and cumin powder and stir.

- Add mince meat and cluster beans and mix well. Sprinkle in remaining ground spices and salt. Pour in one cup water and simmer for 20 minutes till done.

- Stir in vinegar and correct seasoning. Cook till there is just enough liquid to keep mince moist.

Savoury filling 2:

½ cup chick peas (kabuli channa)
2 tbsp oil
1 medium onion, chopped
2 medium tomatoes, chopped
1 tbsp Goa sambar masala
1 tbsp tamarind pulp
Salt to taste

- Boil chick peas till tender.

- Heat oil in a pan and fry onion till soft. Add tomato and cook for 2 minutes. Stir in sambar masala, chick peas, tamarind pulp, salt and one cup water. Simmer till mixture is just moist and not too wet.

To *prepare sandon*:

- Prepare filling of choice.

- Oil or grease a shallow pan that fits into your steamer.

- Pour half the sana batter into pan, spread over filling, and cover with remaining batter.

- Place pan in steamer and cook till a knife inserted comes out clean, about 15-20 minutes.

ODDÉ
Poori

Serves: 4-6

The Goan version of the poori—of course made with toddy.

2 cups whole wheat flour (atta)
1 cup refined flour (maida)
½ cup rice flour
A pinch of salt
1 tsp sugar
2 tbsp ghee (clarified butter) or oil
½ cup toddy
Oil for deep frying

- Place all dry ingredients in a mixing bowl. Mix well. Rub in ghee or oil. Add toddy and enough water to make a firm dough.

- Leave to stand for one hour.

- Knead dough again and roll out to 1/8" thickness.

- Heat oil in a kadahi or deep frying pan. Cut out rounds of dough with a large cutter, about 3-4 inches in diameter and deep fry. Stroke oddé while frying—they should puff out well.

- Drain on paper and serve hot.

- Oddé make a good accompaniment to sorpotel.

COYLOYEO
Rice Flour Griddle Cakes

Serves: 6

Coyloyeo means 'griddle cakes', and they go very well with a xacuti or a meat curry.

3 cups Goa rice, preferably curmot
1 small coconut, grated
4 tsp sugar
1 cup toddy (enough to grind rice and coconut)
½ tsp salt
Ghee (clarified butter) or oil for frying

- Wash rice and soak overnight.

- Drain rice and grind together with coconut and sugar, using toddy. The batter should be of pouring consistency. Add salt. Allow to ferment for 4 hours, for it to rise.

- Heat a griddle or heavy frying pan. Apply a little ghee or oil, and pour on a ladle of batter. Cook one at a time, turning over once to cook on both sides as for pancakes.

APA DE ARROZ
Rice Chapatti

Makes: 8-10 chapatti

These are especially good with a spicy curry.

½ kg (2½ cups) parboiled rice
1 medium coconut, grated
Salt to taste
16-20 square pieces of banana leaves, washed (to fit onto tava)
Ghee (clarified butter) for smearing apa

- Wash rice and soak overnight.

- Grind rice, coconut and salt together, using minimum of water to make a firm but not stiff dough. Knead well.

- Divide dough into 8-10 portions. With wet hands, flatten a portion of dough on a banana leaf square, spreading it evenly to form a thickish chapatti.

- Place tava on medium heat. Place a chapatti on tava, leaf-side down. Cook for 3-4 minutes. Place another leaf on top of chapatti and flip over. Cook till done.

- To serve, remove banana leaves, smear with a little ghee and eat while hot.

CHITIAPS
Rich Rice Pancakes

Makes: 14 pancakes

1½ cup parboiled rice
½ coconut, grated
1 tbsp sugar
2 eggs, beaten
½ tsp baking powder
Salt to taste
¼ cup ghee or vanaspati

- Wash rice and soak overnight.

- Grind rice, coconut and a little water finely, to make a batter of pouring consistency.

- Add sugar, eggs, baking powder and salt. Mix well and cover. Allow to stand for 2 hours.

- Heat a little ghee in a small, heavy frying pan. Pour in 2 tablespoons batter. Cover pan and cook on medium heat for about 2 minutes, when bubbles will appear on surface of pancake.

- Flip over and cook covered, for 1-2 minutes more.

- Make remaining pancakes in the same way.

- Serve with any chicken or meat dish.

APA DE NACHINI
Ragi Flour Chapatti

Makes: 6-8 chapatti

Ragi flour chapatti or bakhri are rich in minerals and very sustaining. Workmen eat them thick and big for lunch, smeared with toope or ghee. A thinner, daintier version is delicious with any vegetable preparation.

2 cups ragi flour
1½ cup water
A pinch of salt
Ghee (clarified butter) or butter for smearing bakhri

- Mix flour, water and salt and knead to make a firm dough, adding more water if necessary. Let it rest for 30 minutes.

- Divide into balls and roll out to desired size and thinness.

- Heat tava, smear with a little ghee or butter and cook bakhri on both sides till done.

- Serve hot.

Desserts

Goans most certainly have a sweet tooth and must have a dessert, however simple, even if it is only a bit of tender coconut and a knob of black jaggery. No festive buffet is complete without at least three desserts, some very elaborate, all rich and luscious.

BEBINCA
Rich Multi-layered Cake

Serves: 14-16

The 'Emperor' of Goan confections, requiring hours of patient labour but earning compliments galore for the cook. The traditional bebinca made of eight coconuts and forty eggs, plus kilos of sugar and pure ghee, boasts about 14-20 delectable layers, each baked to the same golden-brown perfection. Served a slice at room temperature, one could peel off the layers, almost translucent with ghee.

1 large coconut, grated
2¼ cups (450 gm) sugar
1¼ cup (150 gm) refined flour (maida)
Yolk of 8 large eggs
½ tsp salt
Powdered seeds of 8 green cardamoms or ½ tsp grated nutmeg
Slivered almonds
½ kg ghee (clarified butter)
Aluminum pan 6" diameter, 2½" high.

- Grind coconut coarsely and extract one cup thick milk. Add 1½ cup hot water and extract thin milk.

273

- Make a syrup of sugar and water of one thread consistency. Cool to lukewarm.

- Mix flour with thick coconut milk. Add sugar syrup and mix well.

- Beat egg yolks just enough to mix, and add to mixture. Add enough thin coconut milk to make a smooth batter, not too thin. Add salt and powdered cardamom or nutmeg and mix.

- Heat 2 tablespoons ghee in aluminum pan and pour in about one cup batter—just enough to coat bottom of pan. Cover and cook over low heat till set.

- Place pan in preheated oven at 160° (325°C) with only upper heating element on. Bake for 20 minutes till brown. Pour over one tbsp ghee and heat for 2 minutes. Pour in one cup batter, cook, and bake as above. Repeat till all the batter is over. The heat should be medium, to ensure that each layer is thoroughly cooked.

- Cool till lukewarm. Unmould and decorate with slivers of almonds.

DEDOS DE DAMA
Marzipan Lady's Fingers

Serves: 16-18

The brittle caramel coating and the rich Goan version of marzipan make these 'ladies fingers' very kissable indeed! Traditionally, they were served on dainty paper doilies, but presented on sticks they are easier to eat.

3 cups sugar
250 gm peeled almonds, ground in rose water
½ tender, semi-ripe coconut, finely ground
3 egg yolks

- Make a thick syrup with 1½ cup sugar and water.

- Add ground almonds and coconut and mix well.

- Cook for about 5 minutes on medium heat, stirring constantly. Cool to lukewarm.

- Beat yolks just enough to mix and stir into mixture.

- Return to medium heat and cook till mixture leaves sides of pan.

- Cool, enough to handle.

- Divide mixture and roll into 3" fingers. Allow to dry.

- Caramelise remaining sugar by heating it in a pan on medium heat with a minimum of water till it becomes dark brown. Place pan over container of hot water to prevent sugar crystallising.

- Using two forks dip rolled 'fingers' in caramelized

- sugar and place on a lightly oiled surface to cool and dry.

- If desired insert a short stick at one end as a holder.

Desserts

LEITRIA
Tender Coconut and Egg Sweet

Serves 6-8

A very elegant dessert. The lacy covering of egg yolks calls for concentration and patience while cooking.

½ kg (2½ cups) sugar
1 cup water
6 egg yolks
2 cups semi-ripe tender coconuts, grated
100 gm fresh breadcrumbs
50 gm sultanas (kishmish)
50 gm (⅓ cup) peeled almonds or cashew nuts, sliced
2 tsp ghee (clarified butter)
¼ tsp salt
1 tbsp rosewater

- Make a thin syrup with sugar and water, reduce heat and simmer.

- Beat egg yolks to mix well and strain through muslin.

- Stir syrup and using a funnel with a fine hole, rotate funnel and drip about one tablespoon egg yolks slowly into the moving syrup to form a lacy pattern. Cook till set.

- Lift out lacy egg yolk carefully with two forks and set aside on a plate. Repeat with remaining egg yolk.

- Add coconut to syrup with breadcrumbs and a few sultanas and nuts.

- Add ghee and salt and cook on low heat till mixture has absorbed all the syrup.

- Add rose water, stir and turn out on to serving platter. Carefully lift egg 'lace' onto sweet, garnish with remaining sultanas and nuts.

TEIAS DE ARANHA
Cobwebs

Makes: 18-20 pieces

Teias de Aranha is a very delicate looking confection, usually made at Christmas.

The trick is to find a coconut with flesh of the right consistency—tender, yet firm. If it is too soft, it will disintegrate in the syrup.

1 large tender coconut
¼ kg (1¼ cups) sugar
Tissue paper, cut into squares or circles, 3½"-4" wide

- With a sharp knife, remove brown skin of coconut. Drain out water and cut flesh into strips.

- Make a thick syrup with sugar and one cup water. Add coconut strips and cook on low heat, stirring constantly till syrup thickens and begins to crystallise.

- Place pan in a vessel of hot water to prevent syrup from crystallizing completely.

- Working fast, use 2 forks to lift out a few strands of coconut at a time and place on tissue paper. The syrup should not crystallise in the pan.

- Sometimes the syrup is tinted palest pink, green or yellow and the tissue paper is often cut into lacey doilies.

BOLO TATIANA
Nut Cake

Serves: 6-8

The Portuguese probably used pine nuts for this dish, but cashew nuts substitute very well.

1 cup almonds, blanched
1 cup cashew nuts, peeled and roasted
1 cup shelled walnuts
10 eggs, yolks and whites separated
350 gm (1¾ cup) powdered sugar
2 tsp very fine dry breadcrumbs, semolina (rava) or refined flour (maida)
2 tsp rum or brandy
A pinch of salt
Extra breadcrumbs, semolina or flour for dusting baking tin
Icing sugar for dredging top of cake

- Grind all nuts fine.

- Beat egg yolks and sugar till thick and creamy.

- Add breadcrumbs, nuts, rum or brandy and salt. Stir well to mix.

- Beat egg whites till stiff but not dry. Fold into mixture.

- Grease a baking tin and dust with breadcrumbs, semolina or flour.

- Spoon mixture into baking tin and spread evenly.

- Bake in a preheated oven at 190°C (375°F) for 30 minutes. A skewer inserted in the center should come out clean.

- Cool and turn out on a serving dish.
- Decorate with icing sugar dredged through a sieve.

CREPES
Pancakes

Makes: 8-10 pancakes

In Goa, pancakes are delicately thin, just thick enough to hold a filling. The following recipe makes about 8-10 pancakes, and is easily doubled or tripled to yield more.

Filled with sweet tender coconut, they are called ale bele and soaked in a syrup of coconut milk and jaggery, they become guardanapos (napkins).

1 cup refined flour (maida)
1 tsp baking powder
A pinch of salt
1 large egg, beaten
Water to mix
Oil for shallow frying

- Sift flour and baking powder together.

- Stir egg and sufficient water into flour mixture to make 4-5 cups batter. Let it stand for 15 minutes.

- Warm about one teaspoon oil in a heavy frying pan over medium heat. Pour in enough batter, about 1½–2 tbsp, to coat bottom of pan. Cover with lid and cook for about 1½–2 minutes. Turn out on a cool surface.

- Repeat till batter is over.

Note: The pancakes are not flipped over, as they are thin enough to cook when covered.

ALE BELE
Coconut Filled Pancakes

Makes: 8-10 pancakes

Pancakes made as above with 1 cup flour.

Filling:

2 tbsp sugar
1 half-ripe tender coconut, grated
A few sultanas (kishmish) and cashew nuts, chopped
Seeds of 3 green cardamoms, ground, or a good squeeze of lime

- Make a thick syrup with sugar and one tablespoon coconut water. Stir in remaining ingredients.

- Place a little filling along one side of each pancake and roll.

283

GUARDANAPOS
Pancakes in Coconut and Jaggery Syrup

Makes: 8-10 pancakes

Pancakes made as above with 1 cup flour
3 squares (300 gm) Goa palm jaggery
1 coconut, grated
Chopped cashew nuts for garnish

- Crush jaggery and cook with enough water to make a thick syrup. Cool.

- Add 2 cups hot water to coconut and extract thick milk.

- Stir jaggery syrup into coconut milk.

- Arrange pancakes in a dish and pour over syrup. Garnish with chopped cashew nuts.

VELUDO DE COCO
Coconut Velvet

Serves: 6-8

Tinted palest green and set in a pretty mould, serve this dessert with a garland of fresh fruit in season—mangoes, bananas and pineapples, cubed or sliced, or green and black grapes, garnished with fresh mint leaves—and bow to the applause!

2 cups thick coconut milk made from 2 large grated coconuts
3 tbsp gelatine powder
2 cups water
1 tbsp sugar
A few drops almond essence
A few drops green food colouring

Garnish:

Peeled, slivered almonds (optional)
Fresh fruit
Fresh mint leaves

- Put water in a pan, add gelatine and let it soak for 10 minutes.

- Place pan in a double boiler and heat till gelatine dissolves. Add sugar and stir till dissolved. Remove from heat and allow to cool.

- Place gelatine in a large bowl. Place bowl in a container of chipped ice. Using an electric beater, preferably, whip gelatine till light and fluffy.

- Carefully add coconut milk, beating continuously.

- Add essence and colour to obtain a pale green. Pour into a 9" mould and set in refrigerator.

- Unmould carefully onto a dish. Garnish with almonds, fresh fruit and mint leaves and serve.

Garnish:

Peeled, slivered almonds (optional)
Fresh fruit
Fresh mint leaves

PURÉE GELADO DE MANGA
Mango Fool

Serves: 8-10

Semi-ripe mangoes are used for this refreshing summer dessert.

1 kg semi-ripe mangoes
1 tin condensed milk
Powdered sugar to taste
Sprigs of mint for garnish

- Peel and chop mangoes. Discard seeds. Place pulp in a pan with just enough water to cover. Simmer till soft. Allow to cool.

- Mix half mango pulp with half condensed milk in a blender. Repeat with remaining mango and milk. Mix both lots. The mixture should have a thick consistency.

- Add powdered sugar to taste, if needed. It should taste tart and not too sweet.

- Chill and serve in individual bowls, garnished with sprigs of mint.

MOLDE DE MANGADA
Jellied Mango Preserve

Serves 4-6

Serve this made-ahead dessert garnished with fresh sliced mango and mint leaves.

1 cup soft mangada preserve (see recipe)
1 tsp gelatine
1½ cup milk
2 eggs, separated
1 tsp sugar
1 tbsp lime juice

Garnish:

Sliced fresh mango
Mint leaves

- Soak gelatine in ½ cup water.

- Heat milk.

- Beat egg yolks with sugar till creamy.

- Pour in warm milk, stirring to prevent lumps forming. Return to low heat and cook, stirring, till mixture coats back of spoon.

- Remove from heat and cool.

- Stir in mangada and mix thoroughly.

- Heat gelatine till dissolved, cool and add to mixture. Add lime juice and stir.

- Beat egg whites till stiff and fold into mixture.

- Pour mixture into a mould and refrigerate till set.

- Unmould onto a serving dish and garnish with slices of fresh mango and mint leaves.

BEBINCA DE BATATA
Mock Bebinca

Serves: 6-8

Humble cousin of the multi-layered 'emperor' confection, but oh so good to eat, at tea-time or as a dessert!

450 gm (4 medium) potatoes, boiled and mashed
2¼ cups (450 gm) sugar
1½-2 cups milk extracted from 1 large ground coconut
1½ tbsp refined flour (maida), sifted
Yolks of 4 large eggs
Powdered seeds of 6 green cardamoms
2 tsp ghee (clarified butter)

- Mix potatoes, sugar, coconut milk and flour in a blender to make a smooth batter.

- Add egg yolks and cardamom powder. Mix well.

- Heat ghee in a 9" baking mould. Spread ghee around mould. Pour in mixture and bake in preheated oven at 190°C (375°F) for 45 minutes, till brown on top.

- Unmould onto serving dish and serve warm or cold.

EMPADA DE COCO E SEMOLINA
Coconut Pie

Serves: 6-8

Coconut pie is a favourite tea-time snack, but is often served with a custard sauce as dessert.

Filling:

1 cup sugar
1½ cup water
1½ cup semolina (rava)
1 semi-ripe coconut, grated and ground
4 eggs, beaten
1 tbsp grated lime rind

Pastry:

2 cups refined flour (maida)
A pinch of salt
1 tbsp shortening
Water to mix

Filling:

- Make a thin syrup with sugar and water. Cool.

- Stir in semolina and let it stand for 30 minutes.

- Add ground coconut, beaten eggs and lime rind and mix thoroughly.

Pastry:

- Blend flour, salt and shortening till mixture resembles breadcrumbs. Add enough water to make a pliable dough.

To make the pie:

- Roll out dough fairly thin. Grease a 9" pie dish and line with dough. Prick base well and trim off excess pastry. Pour in filling.

- Roll out remaining pastry, cut narrow strips and use to weave a lattice over pie filling. Bake in a preheated oven at 190°C (375°F) for 30 minutes, till set.

Sweets

Every self-respecting Goan housewife always has a plate of doce or sweet preparation to offer the visitor. Necessarily, these preparations keep for quite a few days if not consumed at one go!

DODOL
Coconut and Rice Sweet

Serves: 10-12

Dark brown-black jaggery made from the sap of the coconut tree flower pod gives this sweet its special flavour.

1½ cup raw rice (not parboiled)
2 coconuts
½ kg Goa jaggery
2 tbsp chopped cashew nuts
A pinch of salt
Chopped cashew nuts for garnish (optional)

- Wash rice and soak overnight.

- Grind fine with a little water.

- Grate and grind coconuts coarsely. Extract 4 cups of thick milk, then add 4 cups hot water to extract thin milk.

- Grate jaggery into a pan and mix well with ground rice and thin coconut milk. Place pan on heat and cook till mixture thickens.

- Add thick coconut milk and cook over low heat stirring constantly.

- Add nuts and salt. Continue to cook till mixture leaves sides of pan and oil begins to appear along the edges.

- Pour into a greased flat dish and leave to cool.

- Garnish with a few cashew nuts if desired.

DOCE DE GRÃO
Coconut and Bengal Gram Sweet

Serves: 10-12

A sweet beloved of the young and old alike. Cooked only to a soft stage, it is ideal as a tea-time treat. It can also be cooked to rock-like hardness, when it will keep for weeks in an air-tight tin.

¼ kg (1¼ cup) Bengal gram (channa dal), washed and soaked for one hour
½ kg (2½ cups) sugar
1 half-ripe coconut, grated and finely ground
2 tbsp ghee (clarified butter)
Powdered seeds of 6 green cardamoms
A pinch of salt

- Place dal and 3 cups water in a pan and cook till dal is tender and fairly dry.

- Grind fine.

- Make a fairly thick syrup with sugar and one cup water. Cool till lukewarm.

- Stir in ground dal and coconut and cook over medium heat, stirring constantly.

- As the mixture begins to thicken, add ghee, a spoonful at a time. Keep stirring to prevent sticking.

- When mixture begins to leave sides of pan, add salt and powdered cardamoms.

- Stir well and turn out onto a flat dish. Mark with a knife in a criss-cross design. Allow to cool.

DOCE BAJI
Coconut and Broken Wheat Sweet

Serves: 10-12

Hard to resist, especially for small boys, who have been known to suffer bilious attacks after consuming far too much of this sweet.

½ kg (2 cups) wheat grains crushed coarsely
2 coconuts
½ kg (2½ cups) sugar
½ cup water
2 tbsp ghee (clarified butter)
Powdered seeds of 10 green cardamoms
½ tsp salt

- Wash wheat grains and soak in water for one hour.

- Grate and grind coconuts coarsely. Extract 2 cups thick milk and then 2 cups thin milk.

- Make a syrup of sugar and water.

- Put wheat grains with soaking water and thin coconut milk in a pan and cook till grains are soft.

- Stir in sugar syrup, cooking and stirring all the time. Add thick coconut milk and continue cooking over medium heat.

- Add ghee, a spoonful at a time, then powdered cardamoms and salt. Stir well.

- When mixture begins to leave sides of pan remove from heat and spoon into a greased dish. Cool.

COCADA
Coconut and Semolina Sweet

Serves: 10-12

Made with the ubiquitous coconut, this is a delicious tea-time treat.

1 large semi-ripe coconut, reserve the water and grind flesh fine
¾ kg (3¾ cups) sugar
350 gm (2¼ cups) semolina (rava)
A pinch of salt
Powdered seeds of 8 green cardamoms

- Put sugar and coconut water in a pan and make a syrup, adding plain water to make 4 cups.

- Cool until lukewarm. Add semolina and allow to soak for one hour. Add ground coconut. Place pan on medium heat and cook semolina, stirring continuously.

- When mixture becomes fairly thick, add salt and cardamom powder.

- Continue to cook, stirring continuously, till mixture begins to leave sides of pan.

- Spoon onto a greased platter and cut in diamonds while still warm. Leave to cool.

- This sweet may be cooked softer for immediate consumption, or to a rock-like hardness, when it will keep for a few weeks.

MODAK/PUDDE
Sweet Rice Cones

Makes: 12

The Hindu Goans make these to perfection. The sweet is so highly prized that Lord Ganesh is always shown with a modak in one hand.

2 cups rice
½ tsp salt
½ coconut, grated
½ cup jaggery
Seeds of 3 cardamom, powdered
12 large jackfruit leaves
Ghee to pour over modak

- Wash rice and soak overnight.

- Grind rice with salt and just enough water to make a pliable dough.

- Mix coconut, jaggery and cardamom together.

- Wash jackfruit leaves well and shape into cones. Pin with toothpicks or small sticks.

- Using wet fingers, line each cone with rice dough. Fill with jaggery mixture and cover with more rice dough.

- Bend leaves over to cover contents and tie with string.

- Place modaks in a steamer and cook for 15 minutes till done.

- Remove from leaves.
- Place in a serving dish.
- Pour over melted ghee and serve warm.

CASCA DE CIDRA CRISTALIZADA
Crystallized Citron Peel

Maria Felicia had a citron tree in her backyard that yielded well, and she used the fruit for several purposes. She dispensed the bitter, bitter juice as a tonic for the liver and boiled the rind for the same purpose. She also made the rind into a very acceptable preserve, thank goodness!

The recipe fortunately is not too difficult and can be used for lemon (gulgul), orange and sweet lime, but not for lime.

1 kg citron
1¼ kg (6¼ cups) sugar
25 gm (scant 2 tbsp) sodium bicarbonate

- Wash fruit, cut in quarters, remove pulp and scrape pith off rind. Cut peel into suitable pieces.

- Boil 6 cups water in a pan and add sodium bicarbonate. Stir to dissolve. Add peel and remove pan from heat. Allow to soak for 20 minutes.

- Drain peel, rinse in cold water and cook in fresh water till tender.

- Make a syrup with one kg sugar and 5 cups water. Bring to boil and add peel. Bring to boil again and remove from heat. Place a plate on top to keep peel covered by syrup. Leave to soak for 2 days.

- Drain off syrup. Add ¼ kg sugar to syrup and heat to dissolve sugar. Replace peel. Simmer till peel is transparent. Lift out peel and place on a wire rack, with a tray underneath, to drain.

- Boil syrup till very thick and cloudy. Using tongs, dip each piece of peel into syrup and replace on rack to dry. The syrup should be thick enough to crystallise. When cool and dry, store in an air tight container.

DELICÍA FIGO D'HORTA
Banana Delight

Serves: 6

There is a large yellow variety of banana that grows in Goa. The Portuguese called them Figo d'horta and the prosaic Goans referred to them as sal dathene or thick-skinned. They have a slightly sour taste, which is not unpleasant, and are used for this dish.

6 bananas, just ripe
12 tbsp condensed milk
Juice of 1 large or 2 small limes
Chopped cashew nuts for garnish

- Peel bananas and cut into large pieces.

- Place all ingredients into a food processor and process till reduced to a smooth cream.

- Chill and serve in individual bowls, garnished with chopped cashew nuts.

FIGADA
Banana Preserve

Makes: 6 cups

The floury, huge Moirá bananas are used for this recipe. The preserve is often used as a filling for turnovers with a shortcrust pastry.

4 cups pulp of ripe Moirá bananas
4 cups sugar
1 tsp citric acid crystals

- Put sugar and a little water in a pan over medium heat and make a thick syrup,

- Add banana pulp and citric acid crystals. Cook over medium heat until mixture leaves sides of pan. Stir constantly to prevent sticking.

- Cool and spoon into jars.

MANGADA
Mango Preserve

Makes: 24-25 cups

The ideal mango for this recipe is the monserrat, which is fleshy and ripens late in the season. It can be cooked to softness or firmness by adding less or more sugar. It is most often used as a spread on bread, and is easy to make.

24 cups mango pulp
5 cups sugar
A few cinnamon pieces (optional)
2 tsp citric acid crystals

- Mix mango pulp and sugar in a large pan. Place pan on medium heat and cook, stirring constantly to keep mixture from sticking.

- Add cinnamon and continue cooking till mixture begins to leave sides of pan.

- Remove from heat, cool, add citric acid crystals and stir till dissolved.

- Store in clean jars.

GIRGILADA
Sesame Seed Toffee

Makes: 35-40 diamonds

Cut in diamonds, pale gold, wafer-thin, faintly crisp—a happy blend of honey and sesame seeds, this confection makes any occasion extra special.

750 gm sesame seeds (til)
350 gm (1¾ cup) sugar
1 cup water
6 tbsp honey
1½ tbsp butter or oil

- Heat a tava or griddle on low heat and very lightly toast sesame seeds half a cup at a time.

- Spread butter on a marble slab making a rectangle 12" x 16" in size.

- Divide sesame seeds into 3 portions. Scatter one portion over buttered rectangle.

- Make a syrup of one-thread consistency with sugar and water. Add honey and a second part of sesame seeds. Pour onto rectangle of sesame seeds, taking care not to disturb seeds. Scatter remaining sesame seeds on top.

- With oiled rolling pin, quickly roll toffee into as thin a layer as possible. Cut at once into diamonds, and when cool, store in an air-tight container.

CORDEAL
Almond Toffee

Makes: 1 kg toffee

Made at Christmas and on very special occasions, this pale pink concoction melts in the mouth. Sometimes the almonds are slivered instead of being ground.

4 cups almonds
Rosewater for grinding
3-3½ cups sugar
2 cups water
Pink food colouring

- Soak almonds in hot water for 15 minutes and remove skins. Grind in rosewater.

- Make a thick syrup of sugar and water. Add colour.

- Stir in ground almonds. Cook on low heat till mixture begins to leave sides of pan.

- Pour into buttered pans, 9 " in diameter, 1½ " deep.

- When cool, cut into squares or diamonds.

Note: You may use cashew nuts instead of almonds. Add ½ tablespoon rosewater and a few drops of almond essence with the colouring.

MANDARE
Sweet Papadums of Rice and Pumpkin

Makes: 15-18 papadams

To classify these as 'rice papads' is very misleading. Light-as-air, crisp, delicately flavoured and prettily tinted, they melt in the mouth. This is a Christmas treat requiring a lot of patience to make, but well appreciated.

1½ cup suroi rice or any polished rice (not parboiled)
½ kg red pumpkin (seetaphul or kuddu)
½ cup sugar
½ tbsp sesame seeds (til)

- Wash rice and soak overnight.

- Skin pumpkin, cut into cubes and blanch in slightly salted water.

- Grind rice and pumpkin together to a fine paste with sugar. The paste should not be too thin or too thick.

- Stir in sesame seeds.

- Put ¾ tablespoon of mixture in a saucer and tilt saucer around to spread mixture evenly. The layer should not be too thick or the mandare will be rubbery. Prepare as many saucers as will fit into your steamer, in the same way.

- Bring steamer to boil and steam mandare till they begin to curl at the edges. Remove with a spatula and place on a clean cloth.

- When all mandare have been steamed, lay them out

309

in the sun to dry, for 2-3 days.

- Store in an airtight container.

- When required, deep-fry over medium heat, making sure oil is not too hot, or the mandare will be scorched.

- Serve at once.

MAÇÃPAO
Marzipan

Makes: ¾ kg

My daughter Serena makes perfect marzipan and handles it with confidence, pressing it into moulds and shaping it into Easter eggs. This is her 'no-fail' recipe.

You will need special chocolate or marzipan moulds for this recipe.

Cashew nuts substitute very well for almonds.

250 gm (2½ cups) almonds
500 gm (2½ cups) sugar, powdered
2 egg whites, beaten
1 cup rosewater
Colouring of choice
A few drops almond essence, if using cashew nuts

- Blanch almonds and grind with a little water. Wash grinder with ½ cup water and keep aside.

- Mix almonds, sugar, egg whites, rosewater and almond water in a pan. Cook over low heat until it forms a ball between 2 fingers.

- Remove from heat and allow to cool just enough to handle. Knead well and add essence. It should have the consistency and texture of plasticine.

- If desired, divide marzipan into 2-3 batches and add different colouring to each. Mix well.

- Dust moulds with a little icing sugar. Press marzipan into moulds and leave for 10 minutes. Unmould and

℃

311

allow to dry over night.

- If marzipan is dry and crumbly, grind to a powder, knead with a little rose water and remould. If the mixture is sticky, knead till it is of the right consistency.

BÁTEGA
Coconut Cake

Serves: 8-10

A delectable and easy recipe. The cake is often served for tea.

½ kg (2½ cups) sugar
450 gm (3 cups) semolina (rava)
2 coconuts, ground fine
6 egg yolks
2-3 tbsp ghee (clarified butter)
½ tsp almond essence

- Put sugar and 1½ cup water in a pan and make a syrup.

- Cool. Add semolina and allow to stand for 2 hours.

- Stir in ground coconut.

- Beat yolks to mix well. Stir into mixture alternately with ghee. Add almond essence and stir well. Allow to stand for one hour.

- Pour into greased cake tin and bake in a preheated oven at 190°C (375°F) for 45 minutes, till done.

- Turn out cake. Cool and serve.

BOLINHAS DE MEL
Honey Cakes

Makes: 20-24

Unforgettable are the honey cakes my mother made—a treat reserved for Easter and Christmas. She would not trust the cook, but made them herself; which was quite an undertaking as a lot of patience and time went into the making. As with most Goan recipes, these honey cakes could not be hurried.

The pan used was a special one, with four small cup-like depressions that shaped the cakes into spheres.

4 cups refined flour (maida)
½ tsp salt
1 cup toddy
6 large eggs, lightly beaten
¾ kg (3¾ cups) sugar
½ tsp vanilla essence
Ghee for frying

- Mix flour, salt, toddy and eggs with enough water to make a fairly thick batter.

- Allow to stand for one hour.

- Make a syrup with sugar and one cup water. Cool and add essence.

- Pour a little ghee into each hollow of pan. Carefully drop in a little batter into each hollow. Fry over medium heat till golden, turning cakes once, if necessary.

- Remove cakes from pan, dip into sugar syrup and lift out.

- When all cakes are done, pour over any remaining syrup and serve warm at once.

COSCORÕES
Sweet Shell-shaped Pastries

Makes: 50-60

A Christmas treat, flavoured with almond essence and sometimes tinted palest pink.

1 large coconut
¾ kg (6 cups) refined flour (maida)
2 tbsp ghee (clarified butter)
½ tsp salt
Ghee for deep frying
¾ kg (3¾ cups) sugar
A few drops almond essence
A few drops cochineal colour (optional)

- Grate and grind coconut. Extract 2 cups thick milk.

- Work ghee into flour and add coconut milk and salt. Mix to make a firm dough.

- Roll out fairly thin and cut into 2" squares. Pinch one pair of diagonally opposite corners, together to one side and pinch other 2 corners together to the other side. The resulting shape should look like a sea-shell.

- Heat ghee in a deep frying pan over medium heat, and deep fry a few at a time to a pale gold colour.

- Drain on paper towel.

- Make a two-thread syrup with sugar and water. Add essence and colour, if desired.

- Dip the coscoroes a few at a time into syrup with a slotted spoon. Lift out and spread on a cool surface to dry. The sugar coating should crystallize.

MERENDA

Literally a snack, merenda is the a generic term for a sweet preparation served at tea-time. The ones made with rice and lentils were left to cook slowly on embers during the afternoon siesta.

MERENDA DE BATATA-DOCE
Sweet Potato Merenda

Serves: 4

½ kg sweet potatoes, boiled
4 tbsp coconut, grated
¾ cup palm jaggery, grated
A small pinch of salt
Seeds of 2 green cardamoms, ground

- Peel and slice potatoes. Mix grated coconut and jaggery and toss with sliced potatoes, salt and cardamom powder.

- Serve warm.

OHN
Coconut and Green Bean Sweet

Serves: 8-10

Ohn is a sweet made in celebration of a happy event—the birth of a child, especially a son, an engagement or a wedding. A bowl of ohn would be sent to the neighbours with the announcement.

It is best cooked in a pan over low heat.

6 cups thick milk and 6-7 cups thin milk extracted from 4 large
ground coconuts
1 cup husked green beans (mung dal)
1 cup rice
2½ cups palm jaggery
A good pinch of salt

- Wash dal and rice and soak separately overnight. Drain.

- Place dal, rice and 4 cups water in a large pan. Cook till done.

- Add grated jaggery and thin coconut milk and cook till soft and porridge-like.

- Add thick coconut milk, stir well and serve warm.

Note: Ohn can also be made with Bengal gram (channa dal) in place of green beans.

ATTOL
Merenda of Bengal Gram

Serves 4-6

1 cup fine rice
½ cup husked Bengal gram (channa dal)
1½ cup thick milk extracted from 1 large ground coconut
1 cup palm jaggery, grated
Seeds of 2 green cardamoms, ground
A pinch of salt

- Wash dal and rice and soak for 3-4 hours.

- Drain and put in a pan with 3 cups water. Cook on low heat till soft.

- Add coconut milk and grated jaggery. Continue to cook on a low heat till reduced to a thick consistency.

- Stir in powdered cardamom and salt.

- Serve warm.

MERENDA DE NACHINI
Ragi Merenda

Serves: 4-6

1 cup ragi flour
3 cups water
A pinch of salt
½ tsp fenugreek seeds (methi), ground
1½ cup palm jaggery
2 cups milk extracted from 1 large ground coconut
Powdered seeds of 2 green cardamoms

- Mix ragi flour with water and allow to soak for one hour.

- Place in a pan with salt and cook over low heat stirring constantly to prevent lumps forming.

- Add fenugreek seeds and continue cooking till mixture thickens. Add grated jaggery and coconut milk.

- Continue cooking over low heat for another 3-5 minutes. Stir in cardamom powder and serve warm.

BANANAS DE MOIRÁ ASSADAS
Baked Moirá Bananas

Traditionally baked in banana leaves; foil serves well. The bananas should be semi ripe.

1 banana per person
Butter to brush bananas
Sugar or grated palm jaggery to sprinkle onto bananas

- Preheat oven to 190°C (375°F).

- Wrap each banana in foil and seal carefully.

- Place wrapped bananas on grid of oven and bake for about 10 minutes, turning once during baking.

- Remove wrapping, peel and slice bananas.

- Serve hot brushed with butter and sprinkled with jaggery.

SHEWYO
Steamed Rice Noodles

Serves: 6-8

Noodles made of steamed rice? Could this be the influence of cooks aboard Chinese trading ships? Shewyo has been around for generations and it is far too delicious for us to bother about its origins. It is now a firmly established Goan sweet.

4 cups parboiled Goa rice
A pinch of salt
1 cup thick milk from 1 large coconut
4 squares (400 gm) Goa palm jaggery
¼ tsp powdered seeds of green cardamom (optional)

- Wash rice and soak overnight.

- Grind rice with salt and just enough water to make a firm dough. Allow to rest for one hour.

- Divide dough into medium sized lumps and cook in a steamer for about 20 minutes till done.

- Grate jaggery and dissolve in coconut milk. Add cardamom powder, if using.

- Press into long strings through a potato ricer or sevian machine, while still warm.

- Pour jaggery syrup over shewyo or serve separately.

Relishes, Chutneys & Pickles

RELISHES

Rice and curry, especially fish curry, is usually served with a relish of fresh or salted fish. A simple rice and dal meal is lifted out of the ordinary when eaten with one of these relishes. In the days before the deep-freezer, a monsoon lunch often consisted of Bengal gram (channa dal) cooked with sambar masala and with spicy dried masala Bombay duck as accompaniment. However, one must be warned that roasting or frying salted fish is a highly aromatic exercise!

Roasted Salt Fish

Dried Bombay Duck

- Today these are available already prepared for cooking, either plain or marinated in masala.
- The former can be grilled in a modern oven or soaked and fried with sliced onions and green chillies.

Dried Prawns

- These come in several types, from fine white prawns to larger ones with or without shells.

Dried prawns without shells

- Rinse, drain and dry prawns on paper towel. Pound each prawn lightly to soften flesh.

- Fry plain in oil or apply a little turmeric, chilli powder and vinegar and fry.

Roasted white prawns

- Pick over prawns carefully, rinse and dry on a paper towel.

- Roast on a tava or griddle over low heat till pale gold, stirring constantly to avoid burning prawns.

SPICED WHITE PRAWNS

Makes: 1½ cups

1 medium onion, finely chopped
1 tbsp oil
3 cloves garlic, finely sliced
2 green chillies, deseeded and chopped
¼ tsp turmeric powder
1 cup dried prawns, washed and dried
2 tbsp grated coconut

- Heat oil in a pan and fry onions, garlic and green chillies till onions are golden brown.

- Add turmeric powder. Stir and add prawns and coconut.

- Fry for about 3 minutes, stirring constantly.

CHUTNEYS

CHETNIM DE TOMATO
Tomato Chutney

Makes: 2 kg

Grown in the fields after the rice crop has been harvested,
Goa tomatoes have a tart 'tomato' flavour.

3½ kg ripe but firm tomatoes
1 tsp mustard seeds
125 gm dried red chillies
1 tsp cumin seeds
3 cups vinegar
125 gm garlic
125 gm ginger
3 cups oil
1 tsp fenugreek seeds (methi), ground (optional)
125 gm sugar
Salt to taste

- Chop tomatoes.

- Dry grind mustard seeds.

- Grind chillies and cumin in a little vinegar.

- Finely slice ginger and garlic.

- Heat oil in a pan. Add fenugreek seeds, if using and
  fry for half a minute. Stir in ground masalas. Add
  tomatoes, then ginger and garlic. Cook for 2
  minutes. Add sugar and remaining vinegar. Cook

till thick.

- Add salt to taste.
- Cool and bottle. Store in a cool place.

CHETNIM DOCE DE MANGA
(TIA CARU)
Tia Caru's Sweet Mango Chutney

Makes: 2 kg

Dearly loved by all, especially the younger generation, Aunt Carolina who never married, devoted her life to the comfort of her family. This recipe of hers tastes good as a snack, served on a cracker with grated cheese on top. It keeps very well as no water is used.

1½ kg semi-ripe mangoes, skinned and cut into ½" cubes
1½ kg sugar
50 gm ginger, finely sliced
50 gm garlic, finely sliced
50 gm dry red chillies, finely sliced
1 tsp salt
2 cups vinegar
25 gm (about 20) almonds, peeled and slivered (optional)
25 gm (2 tbsp) sultanas (kishmish) (optional)

- Mix mango cubes with sugar in a pan and cook over low heat till sugar melts. Raise heat to medium and cook till mangoes are translucent.

- Add ginger, garlic and chillies and mix thoroughly. Add salt and half the vinegar and cook for another 5 minutes. The syrup should be thick, clear and golden in colour.

- Correct for consistency and add remaining vinegar and salt as required. It should taste hot, sweet and sour.

- Stir in almonds and sultanas, heat through, and remove from heat.

- Cool completely before bottling.

- Allow to mature for at least 2 weeks.

CHETNIM VERDE
Green Chutney

Makes: 1 cup

A versatile preparation, this is used in sandwiches, on biscuits as a snack, stuffed into fish or served as a relish. A ready aid for the busy housewife, it keeps well in a refrigerator.

2 cups fresh coriander leaves
6-7 green chillies
8 cloves garlic
1½" piece ginger
1 tsp cumin seeds
½ grated coconut
Tamarind the size of a large walnut, with seeds and fibre removed
1 tsp sugar
Juice of 2 limes
Salt to taste

- Place all ingredients in a food processor and grind fine.

- Store in a cool place.

PICKLES

In April and May, before the monsoon breaks, the wise housewife fills large earthenware jars with pickles, from the simple chepnim to the delectable prawn mol and para. These are especially appreciated when fish becomes scarce and expensive.

Like her counterparts the world over, the frugal Goan housewife pickles and preserves in days of plenty so that her family can enjoy fruit, vegetables and fish out of season.

Some of the pickles make an excellent snack spread on hot buttered toast.

PARA
Hot Pickled Salt Fish

Makes: 1½ kg

Every May Angela Mericia went off on a rare visit to the bazaar, to select carefully the salt fish for para—it was a task not to be entrusted to the cook. She bought surmai, thick with salt, oozing fat and firm to the touch. The para was for the monsoon months ahead, when fish was very, very scarce and very, very expensive.

After all the fish in the para was eaten, the leftover marinade was added to fried onions and made a fantastic topping on hot buttered toast.

1½ kg salted kingfish (surmai)
2 litres 'strong' vinegar
25 gm garlic, ground
25 gm ginger, ground
350 gm red 'button' chillies, powdered
2 tbsp cumin powder
2 tbsp turmeric powder
1 tbsp powdered curry leaves, which have been dried in the sun

- Debone and cut fish into 1½" long pieces. (Reserve the centre bone for a curry made with small aubergines). In a ceramic or steel vessel, wash fish in vinegar till free of sand.

- Strain this vinegar through double muslin and mix with ginger, garlic, chilli, cumin and turmeric powders.

- Place fish in a large jar and pour in spice mixture. Cover jar and leave overnight.

- The next day add more vinegar as fish will have absorbed the marinade.

- Sprinkle on powdered curry leaves and replace cover.

- Leave to mature for at least 3 weeks.

To serve:

- Put 2 tablespoons water in a frying pan and spoon in 1-2 pieces of para. Simmer on low heat till liquid has dried. Pour in a little oil and fry fish pieces.

MÔL DE CAMARÃO
Prawn Pickle

Makes: 1½ kg

This was Marie Felicia's special recipe. The prawns have to be large and very fresh, else the pickle will spoil.

1½ kg prawns, peeled, cleaned, deveined and lightly salted
½ tsp cumin powder
6 cloves
8 peppercorns
3" piece whole turmeric
½ pod garlic
4" piece ginger
Seeds of 4 green cardamoms
3" piece cinnamon
10 dried red Kashmiri chillies
2 cups vinegar
Salt to taste
Sesame seed oil for shallow frying

- Grind all spices with a little vinegar. Mix in remaining vinegar, place in a pan and cook over low heat, adding salt to taste. Cool thoroughly.

- Heat oil in a frying pan. Trim prawns and fry carefully. Cool on a large plate.

- Pour masala and vinegar sauce into a wide-mouthed jar. Carefully immerse prawns, making sure they are well below level of vinegar.

- Place jar in a cool place, and allow mol to mature for at least 5 days.

BALCHÃO DE CAMARÃO - I
Prawn Balchao

Makes: 2 cups

This pickle is best made with tiny dried prawns with shells, and is delicious with hot buttered toast.

½ kg very small dried prawns with shells, carefully picked over
2 cups + 3tbsp vinegar
2 cups oil
6 onions, chopped
A few curry leaves
1 kg (12 large) tomatoes, chopped
3 tbsp sugar
Salt to taste

Finely ground with a little vinegar:
125 gm ginger
1 pod garlic
50 gm dried red Kashmiri chillies

- Wash prawns and soak overnight in 2 cups vinegar. Mince in a food processor almost to a paste.
- Heat oil in a pan and fry onions till brown. Add curry leaves and stir. Add ground spices and fry for a few minutes till oil separates.
- Add tomatoes, sugar and salt to taste. Cook for 10 minutes.
- Add prawns and 3 tablespoons vinegar and cook till dry.
- Cool and fill into air-tight jars.
- Allow to mature for one week.

BALCHÃO DE CAMARÃO - II
Prawn Balchao
Makes: 750 gm

A 'quick and easy' recipe which also keeps well.

100 gm tiny, dried prawns with shells
2 pods garlic, ground
2 tsp turmeric powder
2 tsp cumin powder
2 tsp mustard powder
1 cup vinegar
1 cup oil
¾ kg (6 large) onions, finely chopped
3 tsp sugar
1 tbsp chilli power
1 tbsp salt

- Pick over prawns to clean. Rinse well and dry in the sun.

- Mix spices to a paste in a little vinegar and leave for 30 minutes to blend.

- Heat oil in a pan and fry onions till pale brown. Stir in masala, sugar and salt. Fry well on low heat.

- Add prawns and continue cooking and stirring to prevent mixture sticking to pan.

- Stir in remaining vinegar and cook till it is absorbed. The mixture should be moist.

- Cool and fill into clean jars.

- Allow to mature for one week.

MANGUINHAS EM ÁGUA E SAL
CHEPNIM
Mango Water Pickle

100 tender small green mangoes with soft seeds
1 tsp asafoetida powder (hing)
2 tbsp mustard seeds
1½ kg sea salt
10 large dried red chillies
2 tbsp fenugreek seeds (methi)

- Wash and dry mangoes.

- Mix all ingredients except mangoes and salt.

- Place some salt at the bottom of a large enameled, china or glass pan. Put a layer of mangoes on salt and top with spices. Repeat layers ending with salt.

- Place a small plate with a 6-8 kg weight over pickle. Cover mouth of pan with a thick cloth and tie securely.

- After 3 days, remove weight and turn mangoes so that the lower ones are on top.

- The mangoes will have exuded quite a bit of fluid. Replace weight and cloth and leave for a further 4 days.

- Carefully transfer pickle to clean dry jars, making sure the brine covers the mangoes.

- Allow to mature for 8-10 days.

Note: The mangoes should be about 2" long.

MISCUT
Hot Mango Pickle

50 tender green mangoes
1 kg salt
2 tbsp turmeric powder
6 cups sesame seed (til) oil
2 tbsp fenugreek (methi) seeds
1" piece whole turmeric
1" piece whole asafoetida (hing)
10 tbsp mustard seeds
10 tbsp chilli powder

- Wash and thoroughly wipe mangoes dry. Cut into cubes, discarding seeds.

- Sprinkle over salt and turmeric powder. Mix well. Place in a large container cover with a plate and place a 6-8 kg weight on top. Keep for 2 days, stirring once a day.

- Heat oil in pan till smoking. Put in fenugreek seeds, whole turmeric and asafoetida and remove from heat before spices burn. Lift out spices and allow to cool.

- Replace oil on heat. Add 5 tablespoons mustard seeds and remove from heat. Allow to cool.

- Lightly roast remaining mustard seeds and grind.

- Dry grind fried asafoetida, turmeric and fenugreek seeds.

- Add chilli powder and all spices to oil.

- Drain mango pieces. Reserve liquid.

- Add mango to oil and spice mixture. Stir well to coat all mango pieces.

- Pack pieces of mango in clean dry jars. Pour over reserved mango water, making sure liquid level is above mangoes. Seal well and allow to mature for 10-14 days.

ACHAR DE LIMÃO PICANTE
Lime Pickle

The limes in this pickle take on a pale apricot colour while the sun does the cooking. The perfect recipe for the busy housewife.

> 75 limes, fresh and thin-skinned
> 8 tbsp sugar
> 6 tbsp salt
> 2 tbsp chilli powder

- Wash limes and dry well.

- Squeeze out juice of 25 limes. Strain and keep aside.

- Cut remaining limes across into halves. Layer limes, sugar, salt and chilli powder in a large clean dry jar. Shake and tilt jar, while filling, to mix spices with lime. Pour over lime juice. Cover jar and place in the sun for 14 days. Shake and tilt jar twice a day.

- Store in a cool place for one week before using.

- This should last for one year.

ACHAR DE LIMÃO DOCE
Sweet and Sour Lime Pickle

Makes: 2 cups

After making Xarope de Limão (see recipe), the frugal housewife makes a pickle from the lime skins, and it is good.

Skin of 24 limes, cut into pieces
½ tbsp salt
8 cups water
1½ cups sugar
2 cups vinegar
12 cloves garlic, sliced
2" piece ginger, sliced
1 tbsp chilli powder

- Apply salt to lime skins and keep aside for one hour.

- Put lime skins and water into a pan and cook till tender. Drain.

- Place sugar and vinegar in another pan and dissolve sugar over medium heat. Add garlic, ginger and chilli powder. Cook on low heat for 10 minutes.

- Add lime skins and cook for a further 10 minutes. Correct seasoning, adding more sugar, vinegar or salt as desired.

- Cool and fill into clean dry jars. Store in a cool place and allow to mature for at least 15 days.

ACHAR DE BERINGELAS
Aubergine Pickle

Makes: 1 kg

A fairly mild pickle, delicious with hot parantha!

1½ kg medium sized seedless aubergines, washed and well dried
1½ tbsp salt
3" piece ginger
2 pods garlic
15 to 20 dried red chillies
2 cups vinegar
1½ cup oil
1 tbsp mustard seeds
3 tbsp sugar

- Wash aubergines and cut into cubes. Mix in salt and leave for 30 minutes.

- Grind ginger, garlic and chillies in vinegar.

- Put oil in a pan and heat. Add mustard seeds, and when they stop popping add ground masala and fry well.

- Add aubergines together with brine that will have formed, sugar and remaining vinegar. Cook till the gravy is thick.

- Cool and bottle.

ACHAR DE TENDLIM
Tendli Pickle

Makes: 1 kg

This small gherkin-like vegetable grows profusely during the monsoon and once picked, ripens fast. Discard any with even a hint of orange inside, they will spoil the pickle.

¾ kg tendli, washed and well dried
2 tsp salt
1 tbsp chilli powder
½ tsp fenugreek powder (methi)
½ tbsp turmeric powder
2" piece ginger, ground
1 pod garlic, ground
1½ cup oil
2 cups vinegar
½ cup sugar

- Cut tendli into 4 length-wise. Mix with salt and leave for 3 hours.

- Mix together next 5 ingredients.

- Heat oil in a pan, lower heat and fry spice mixture for 2 minutes.

- Stir in vinegar and bring to boil. Add sugar and stir till dissolved.

- Add tendli, lower heat and cook till tender. Do not overcook.

- Cool and bottle.

ACHAR DE BILIMBINS
Bimblee pickle

Makes: 1½ kg

Bimblees are small cucumber-like fruit that hang in bunches on the tree trunk.

They are crisp and very tart, and are often used in fish curries, either fresh or dried.

1 kg bimblees
3 tbsp salt
2 cups oil
1 tbsp chopped curry leaves
1 tbsp chilli powder
¼ kg jaggery
½ cup vinegar
¼ cup almonds
¼ cup sultanas (kishmish)

Finely ground:

3" piece ginger
2 small pods garlic

- Cut bimblees into 4, mix with salt and leave for 4 hours.

- Heat oil in a pan and fry curry leaves.

- Lower heat, add chilli powder, ginger and garlic and fry well.

- Squeeze out liquid from bimblees and add to pan.

- Dissolve jaggery in vinegar and stir into mixture.

Keep heat low.

- Add almonds and sultanas and cook till oil floats to top.

- Cool and bottle.

Beverages

ORCHATA
Almond Sherbet

Makes: 1½ litres

A sherbet reserved for very special occasions, expensive but very refreshing. Did the recipe come from the Moors via the Portuguese, or was it 'stolen' from Adil Shah's cohorts!

500 gm almonds
250 gm (1¼ cup) sugar
1 tsp rosewater (optional)

- Blanch almonds and remove skins.

- Grind in liquidiser in 3 or 4 portions, adding enough water to make a thin purée-like paste.

- Strain through a fine muslin cloth. Mix about ¾ litre more water into paste to extract maximum liquid.

- Make a syrup with sugar and one litre water, cooking it to a one thread consistency.

- Pour in almond liquid and cook till thickened, taking care to keep stirring. The syrup should be thick but of pouring consistency.

- Add rosewater if desired.

- Cool and fill into bottles.

- Serve diluted with water and crushed ice.

- It will keep in the refrigerator for 2 weeks.

XAROPE DE LIMÃO
Lime Sherbet

Makes: 3 litres

There is a variety of lime in Goa that is large, thin-skinned and pale orange in colour. It has a slightly different flavour from the regular lime.

The syrup keeps well and is a popular summer drink, especially with a tot of feni!

100 limes
¾ kg (3 ¾ cups) sugar
1 ¾ litre water

- Squeeze limes to extract one litre juice. Strain carefully.

- Make a syrup with sugar and water to a one thread consistency. Strain and cool.

- Stir in lime juice and bottle.

- Keep in a cool place.

- Dilute with water and serve with a crushed lime leaf.

- It will keep for 1-2 months.

XAROPE DE BRINDÃO
Kokum Syrup

Makes: 1½-2 litres

The brindão is the kokum, well-known and widely used in Deccani and west coast cooking. The syrup becomes a deep ruby-red. It is tart and very refreshing on a hot summer's day, served over crushed ice.

100-150 large, ripe, fleshy kokum fruit, freshly picked
1½ kg sugar
¾ litre water

- Wash fruit and blanch.

- Cut fruit in half and remove pulp and seeds. Mince skins coarsely.

- Strain as much juice as possible first from the pulp then from the skins through a fine muslin cloth. Mix both juices.

- Make a fairly thick syrup of sugar and water over medium heat.

- Cool slightly and add juice. Cool thoroughly and bottle.

- It will stay for 1-2 months.

VINHO DE GENGIBRE
Ginger Wine

Makes: 3-4 litres

Non-alcoholic, sipped both as appetizer and digestive, easy to make, this 'wine' satisfies both the palate and the conscience of the teetotaller. (But the addition of a peg of brandy to a bottle of wine cheers things up no end!)

¼ kg ginger, well ground
4½ litres water
5-6 red chillies, deseeded
5 green cardamoms
8 cloves
5" piece cinnamon, broken into bits
Juice of 4 large limes
¾ kg (3¾ cups) sugar
1 tsp citric acid crystals

- Mix together all spices, ginger and water in a pan and bring to boil, then simmer for one hour.

- Stir in lime juice and cook for 15 minutes more. Strain through a muslin cloth.

- Caramelize 2 tablespoons sugar by heating in a pan with a little water till it turns brown. Add to strained liquid.

- Add remaining sugar and stir till dissolved. Return pan to heat and simmer for 30 minutes more.

- Remove from heat and when lukewarm, stir in citric acid crystals. Add more sugar if required.

- Cool and bottle. It will keep for about 3 months.

VINHO DE SEIVA DE COQUEIRO
Toddy Wine

Makes: 3 litres

A fairly good imitation Muscatel, the light sweet wine favoured by genteel ladies of the last century, its pale look belies the high alcohol content. The toddy must be fresh, or the wine will spoil.

½ kg large black raisins
4 bottles, sweet toddy
¾ kg (3 ¾ cups) sugar
Juice of 2 large limes

- Wash raisins well and dry in the sun. Pass through a mincer

- Mix toddy, sugar and lime-juice in a large jar. Stir till sugar is dissolved. Add chopped raisins and mix thoroughly.

- Tie a thick cloth over mouth of jar. Keep in a dark place, stirring mixture once every day for 8 days. Leave untouched for a further 2 days.

- On the 11th day strain through a double muslin cloth, and bottle.

- To darken the colour, mix in 4 tablespoons burnt sugar.

- 'The longer it is kept the better it tastes.'

Glossary

English	Portuguese	Konkani	Hindi
Almond	Amendoas	Amena	Badam
Aubergine	Beringelas	Vaingon	Baingan
Baked	Refugada	Refugada	—
Baking Powder	Fermento em po	—	Meetha soda
Bay Leaf	Folhos de loura	Tez patha	Taj patta
Beef	Bife	Ghaichem maas	Badda ka gosht
Bitter Gourd	Caratins	Caratins	Karela
Black-eyed beans	—	Virvil	Lobia ki phalli
Brain	Miolhos	Beja	Bheja
Bread	Pao	Pao	Double roti
Bread crumbs	Migalhas	—	—
Butter	Manteiga	Mosko	Makhan
Cabbage	Repolho	Repolho	Band gobi
Capsicum	Pimento	Mote misango	Simla mirch
Cardamom	Cardomomo	Elichi	Elaichi
Carrot	Cenoura	Gazor	Gajar
Cauliflower	Couveflor	Phulgobi	Phool gobi
Celery	Aipo	—	—
Cheese	Queijo	Zueijo	—
Chicken	Galinha	Combi	Murgh
Cinnamon	Canela	Tikki	Dalchini
Clam	Ameijoas	Tisreos	Tisri
Clove	Cravos	Kalafuram	Laung

English	Portuguese	Konkani	Hindi
Coconut	Coco	Naal	Nariyal
Conjee	Peize	Peize	Kanji
Coriander	Cilantro	Cothmir	Dhania
Cornflour	Maisena	—	—
Crabs	Carangue jos	Couleo	Kenkada
Cumin	Cominho	Jeerem	Jeera
Drumstick	Moringueiro	Moxing	Sojni ki phalli
Egg	Ovo	Tantia	Anda
Fat/lard	Gordura	—	Charbi
Fenugreek	Fenacho	Methi	Methi
Fish	Peixe	Nishtem	Machchi
Flour	Farinha	Peel	Maida
Fowl/chicken	Galinha	Combi	Murgh
Fritters	Boje	Boje	Pakora
Garlic	Alhos	Loson	Lehsun
Ginger	Gengibre	Alem	Adrak
Green chilli	Malangueta	Misango	Hari Mirch
Ham	Presunta	Presunta	—
Ham (leg)	Perna	—	Raan
Indian flat bread	Apa	Bakhri	Roti
Indian fried bread	Odde	Poori	Poori
Indian sour plum			
—dried	Solan	Solan	Kokum
—fresh	Brindão	Bhindim	Kokum
Lentils	Lentilha	Dal	Dal
Lime	Limão	Limão	Nimbu
Liver	Figado	Caiz	Kaleji
Lobster	Lagosta	—	Bada jhinga
Macaroni	Macarrao	Macarrao	Macroni
Mackeral	Cavalas	Bangda	Bangda
Morello cherry	Bilimbi	Bimblee	—
Mussels	Meixilhaos	Shinaneo	—
Nutmeg	Noz-moscada	Zaiphul	Jaiphul
Oil	Oleo	Tel	Tel
Olive oil	Azeita de oliveira	Azeitachem tel	Jaitun tel
Onion	Cebola	Kando	Pyaz
Oyster	Ostras	Calvan	Kaloo

English	Portuguese	Konkani	Hindi
Patties/Balls	Almondegas	Almondegas	Kabab
Peppercorn	Pimenta	Mirem	Kali mirch
Pie/Small pies	Empada/ empadinha	—	—
Poppy seed	Semente de papoila	Cuscus	Khuskhus
Potato	Batata	Botate	Alu
Prawn	Camerão	Sungtam	Jhinga
Pullet	Frango	Pil	Murgh
Pungent	Picante	Teek	Teekha
Red pumpkin	Abóbora	Tambdo Dudi	Kaddu/Sitaphul
Rice	Arroz	Tandul/sheeth	Chawal
Ridged gourd	Goncalim	Goncallim	Touri
Roast	Assada	Assada	—
Salt	Sal	Meet	Namak
Salted	Salgada	Kharem	Namkeen
Sausage	Chouriço	Chouriço	—
Semolina	Semola de trigo	Sooji	Rava
Snake gourd	Podollim	Podollim	Chirchinda
Soup	Sopa	Sopa	Shorva
Spare ribs	Caril de Ossos	Aadmaas	Seena
Stuffed	Recheada	Recheada	—
Stuffing	Recheio	Recheio	—
Suckling	Leitao	Leitao	Chota suvar
Sugar	Acucar	Sakor	Cheeni
Syrup	Xarope	Xarope	Sharbat
Tartlet forms	Forminhas	—	—
Toddy	Seiva de palmeira	Sura	Tadi
Tomato	Tomate	Tomatam	Tamatar
Tongue	Lingua	Gibe	Zaban
Turmeric	Acafrao da India	Olod	Haldi
Vanilla	Baunilha	Vanille	—
Vinegar	Vinagre	Inagre	Sirka
Walnut	Noz	—	Akhroat
Wine	Vinho	Vine	—

References

Inside Goa by Manohar Malgaonkar
India and the West by Joseph Velinkar
Goa by Mario Cabral e Sa
Palaces of Goa by Helder Carita
A Kind of Absence by João da Veiga Coutinho
Essays on Goan History by Fatima Gracias

Index

APPETIZERS

Beef
 – Croquettes (Rissoles), 72
 – Pasteis favoritos (Favourite patties), 70

Fish
 – Fofos (Fish rolls), 51

Lentil
 – Boje (Nuggets of Bengal gram), 74

Mussel
 – Forminhas com mexilhões (Mussel tartlets), 64

Oyster
 – Pasteis de ostras (Oyster patties), 61

Pork
 – Empadinhas (Little pork pies), 67
 – Pão com choriço (Goa sausage burgers), 73

Prawn
 – Almondegas de camarão (Prawn cakes), 57
 – Paparis recheados (Stuffed papads), 59
 – Rissóis de camarão (Prawn turnovers), 55
 – Torradas de camarão (Prawn toasts), 53

BEEF

Assado de bife (Roast beef), 173

Bife com cebolas (Onion steaks), 171

Bife enrolado (Rolled beef), 174

Curries
- Bife à pais de Goa (Goa country-style beef), 168
- Bife bafad (Thick beef curry), 170
- Bolinhas de carne em caril verde (Meatballs in green curry), 164
- Caril de bife (Curried beef), 166

Enrolados de bife (Beef rolls), 176

Mince
- Beringelas recheadas (Stuffed aubergines), 237
- Bolinhas de carne em caril verde (Meatballs in green curry), 164
- Carne picante com batata-doce (Savoury mince with sweet potatoes), 162
- Casserole de carne (Baked mince with potatoes), 163
- Pao recheado com carne picada (Stuffed mince loaf), 160
- Podollim recheado com carne picada (Snake gourd stuffed with mince), 231

Tongue
- Guizado de Lingua à Tia Anu (Stewed tongue a la Tia Anu), 178
- Lingua assada em pote (Pot-roasted tongue), 180

BEVERAGES

Orchata (Almond sherbet), 351

Vinho de gengibre (Ginger wine), 354

Vinho de seiva de coqueiro (Toddy wine), 355

Xarope de brindão (Kokum syrup), 353

Xarope de limão (Lime sherbet), 352

BREADS

Apa de arroz (Rice chapatti), 268

Apa de nachini (Ragi flour chapatti), 270

Chitiaps (Rich rice pancakes), 269

Coyloyeo (Rice flour griddle cakes), 267

Oddé (Poori), 266

Sana (Steamed rice cakes), 261

Sandon (Steamed rice cakes with savoury or sweet filling), 263

CHICKEN

Assado de galinha com chouriço de reino (Roast chicken with Portuguese sausage), 148

Curries
  – Caril de galinha (Chicken curry), 141
  – Estew à Maria Felicia (Maria Felicia's chicken stew), 139
  – Galinha à Alzira (Alzira's chicken), 145
  – Xacuti de galinha (Chicken curry), 143

Frango Veneciana (Chicken Venician), 151

Frango Vera (Chicken Vera), 146

Galantine de galinha (Galantine of chicken), 153

Galinha cafreal (Chicken barbecue), 150

Galinha picante à Angela Mericia (Spicy chicken a la Angela Mericia), 147

CHUTNEYS

Chetnim de tomato (Tomato chutney), 330

Chetnim doce de manga (Tia Caru's sweet mango chutney), 332

Chetnim verde (Green chutney), 334

CLAMS

Ameijoas com coco (Clams with coconut), 130

CRABS

Caranguejos recheados (Stuffed crab), 128

Caril de caranguejos (Crab curry), 126

CRAYFISH

Xeq xeq (Thick crayfish or lobster curry), 124

DESSERTS

Ale bele (Coconut filled pancakes), 283

Bebinca (Rich mult-layered cake), 273

Bebinca de batata (Mock bebinca), 290

Bolo Tatiana (Nut cake), 280

Crepes (Pancakes), 282

Dedos de dama (Marzipan lady's fingers), 275

Empada de coco e semolina (Coconut pie), 291

Guardanapos (Pancakes in coconut and jaggery syrup), 284

Leitria (Tender coconut and egg sweet), 277

Molde de Mangada (Jellied mango preserve), 288

Puré gelado de manga (Mango fool), 287

Teias de aranha (Cobwebs), 279

Veludo de coco (Coconut velvet), 285

FISH

Almondegas de peixe (Fish cakes), 102

Bacalhau (Portuguese salt cod with dried beans), 111

Barrada de peixe (Curried fish—Daman style), 99

Cavalas fumadas em feno (Smoked mackerel), 109

Curries
 – Ambot-tik (Hot and sour fish curry), 95
 – Caldeirada (Mild fish curry), 91
 – Caldinho (Mild fish curry), 89
 – Caril de peixe (Fish curry), 93

Filetes enroladas de cação ou raia (Rolled fillet of baby shark or skate fish), 103

Fritada de peixe (Fried fish in gravy), 101

Peixe à Portuguesa (Fish-Portuguese style), 97

Peixe recheados (Stuffed fried fish), 108

Peixe recheado com tempero verde (Whole fish with green masala), 104

Peixe serra temperado (Spiced whole kingfish), 106

Salada de cavalas salgadas (Salad of salted mackerel), 110

LOBSTER

Xeq xeq (Thick crayfish or lobster curry), 124

MASALA

Bafad masala, 47

Recheio masala, 46

Sambar masala, 47

MUTTON

Brain
  – Almondegas de miolo (Brain cutlets), 186
  Liver
  – Figado com cebolas (Liver with onions), 184
  – Iscas (Stir fried liver), 182

Xacuti de cameiro (Mutton curry), 157

OYSTERS

Empada de ostras à Tia Rubertina (Tia Rubertina's oyster pie), 132

PICKLES

Achar de beringelas (Aubergine pickle), 345

Achar de bilimbins (Bimblee pickle), 347

Achar de tendlim (Tendli pickle), 346

Lime
  – Achar de limão doce (Sweet and sour lime pickle), 344
  – Achar de limão picante (Lime pickle), 343

Mango
  – Manguinhas em água e sal chepnim (Mango water pickle), 340
  – Miscut (Hot mango pickle), 341

Para (Hot pickled salt fish), 335

Prawn
- Balchão de camarão – I (Prawn balchao), 338
- Balchão de camarão – II (Prawn balchao), 339
- Môl de camarão (Prawn pickle), 337

PORK

Carne de porco em 'marinada branca' (Pork with feni), 206

Carne de porco salgada (Salted pork), 211

Costeletas de porco em feni (Pork chops in feni), 210

Curries
- Aadmaas (Meat bone curry), 203
- Cabidela (Curried pigling), 201
- Peet-achem maas (Savoury pork stew), 204
- Sarapatel (Spicy curry of pork and liver), 199
- Vindalho (Spicy pork curry), 197

Roasts
- Assado de porco (Pot roast of pork), 193
- Leitão assado (Roast suckling), 190
- Pernas de leitão assado (Roast suckling hams), 195

Porco com castanhas de jaca (Pork with jackfruit seeds), 209

Sausages
- Chouriço de Goa (Goa sausage), 214
- Chouriço do reino (Portuguese sausages), 217
- Feijoada (Goa sausages with dried beans), 216

Tamreal de porco (Pork stew), 208

Trotters
- Pés de porco temperados (Trotters), 213

PRAWNS

Apa de camarão – I (Prawn cake), 120

Apa de camarão – II (Prawn cake), 122

Camerão com cebolas (Prawns with onions), 115

Camarão 'tigre' frito (Fried tiger prawns), 114

Caril de camarão (Prawn curry), 113

Empada de camarão (Prawn pie), 117

Prawns with vegetables
- Abóbora com camarão (Red pumpkin with prawns), 227
- Beringelas recheadas (Stuffed aubergines), 237
- Caldinho de abóbra branca com camarão (Mild curry of white pumpkin with prawns), 230
- Caratins recheados com camarão (Bitter gourd stuffed with prawns), 241
- Podollim recheado com camarão (Snake gourd stuffed with prawns), 231
- Suquem de beringelas com camarão seco (Savoury aubergines with prawns), 237

RELISHES

Roasted salt fish

- Dried Bombay duck, 327

- Dried prawns, 327

- Dried prawns without shells, 327

- Roasted white prawns, 328

Spiced white prawns, 329

RICE

Arroz à Portuguesa (Pulau—Portuguese style), 257

Arroz com coco (Coconut rice), 251

Arroz de camarão (Prawn pulau), 255

Arroz refogado (Baked rice pulau), 253

SOUPS
Chicken
 – Caldo de galinha (Chicken broth), 80
 – Sopa grossa (Minestrone—Goan style), 82
Prawn
 – Sopa de camarão (Prawn soup), 77
 – Sopa de camarão e batata (Prawn soup with potatoes), 79
Vegetable
 – Caldo verde (Spinach soup), 84
 – Sopa de repolho (Cabbage soup), 85

SQUID
Lulas guizadas do Algarve (Curried squid a la Algarve), 134
Lulas recheadas (Stuffed Squid), 135

SWEETS
Bátega (Coconut cake), 313
Bolinhas de mel (Honey cakes), 314
Casca de cidra cristalizada (Crystallized citron peel), 302
Cocada (Coconut and semolina sweet), 299
Cordeal (Almond toffee), 308
Coscorões (Sweet shell-shaped pastries), 316
Delicia figo d'horta (Banana delight), 304
Doce baji (Coconut and broken wheat sweet), 298
Doce de grão (Coconut and gram sweet), 297
Dodol (Coconut and rice sweet), 295

Figada (Banana preserve), 305

Girgilada (Sesame seed toffee), 307

Maçãpao (Marzipan), 311

Mandare (Sweet papadums of rice and pumpkin), 309

Mangada (Mango preserve), 306

Merenda
  – Attol (Merenda with Bengal gram), 320
  – Bananas de Moirá assadas (Baked Moirá bananas), 322
  – Merenda de batata-doce (Sweet potato merenda), 318
  – Merenda de nachini (Ragi merenda), 321
  – Ohn (Coconut and green bean sweet), 319
  – Shewyo (Steamed rice noodles), 323

Modak/pudde (Sweet rice cones), 300

VEGETABLES

Agsal (Pepper Water), 247

Aubergine (baingan)
  – Beringelas fritas (Fried sliced aubergine), 235
  – Suquem de beringelas (Savoury aubergines), 236

Bitter gourd (Karela)
  – Caratins picantes (Spicy bitter gourd), 238
  – Caratins recheados com batata-doce (Bitter gourd stuffed with sweet potatoes), 240

Black-eyed beans (lobia)
  – Melgor (Black-eyed beans with coconut), 244

Cabbage (bund gobi)
  – Fugad de repolho (Savoury cabbage with coconut), 223
  – Salada de repolho (Cabbage salad), 232

Caldinho de lugumes (Mild vegetable curry), 90

Cluster beans (gwar phalli)
 – Fugad de chitkeo mitkeo (Savoury cluster beans with coconut), 223

Coconut kokum curry, 248

Drumsticks (sojni ki phalli)
 – Fugad de xengo (Savoury drumsticks with coconut), 224

French beans (farash beans)
 – Fugad de feijão verde (French beans with coconut), 223

Jackfruit (kathal)
 – Preparado picante de jaca verde (Curried jackfruit), 242

Okra (bhindi)
 – Mergol de quiabos (Okra—Portuguese style), 225

Red amaranthus (cholai)
 – Tambadi bhaji (Savoury red amaranthus), 221

Red pumpkin (kuddu or seetaphul)
 – Mergol de abóbora (Red pumpkin—Portuguese style), 225
 – Suquem de abóbora – I (Savoury red pumpkin), 226
 – Suquem de abóbora – II (Savoury red pumpkin), 227

Ridged gourd (touri)
 – Mergol de gosaim (Ridged gourd—Portuguese style), 225

Snake gourd (chirchinda)
 – Podollim recheado com batata-doce (Snake gourd stuffed with sweet potatoes), 231

Sorak (Curry sauce), 246

Sweet potato (sakarkand)
 – Batata-doce picante (Savoury sweet potatoes), 234

White pumpkin (petha)
 – Caldinho de abóbora branca (White pumpkin curry), 229

White radish (safed mooli)
 – Fugad de rabanete (White radish with coconut), 223

Ragout de haricot (Haut)...
Feijão de Chicoeurinho Savory dinner beans with bacon[?], 224

Marinat Kobau vuert... 86

Drumsticks (pinti kabilli)...
Sapade de courge hairy drumsticks with coconut, 224

Whitebeans (haricot...)
Feijão de igot verde (French bean stew with coconut), 223

Escabeut (fruit)...
Escabeut do puerro de gatz verde (Cru led jam fruit), 242

Okra (Gumbo)...
A(r)rôz de gumbo (Okra — Portuguese style), 228

Red tamarind re-(colin)...
Tamuru bhaji (savoury red tamarind stem), 221

Red pumpkin (kath, orange phal)...
Bulol de abobora (Red pumpkin — Portuguese style), 225
Sopinha de abobora — (Savoury red pumpkin), 226
Saqu(t) de abobora — (Savoury red pumpkin), 227

Baked ground (root)...
Metropoli de gesto (Baked ground — Portuguese style), 214

Snake gourd (Chuchhu)...
Pinosinta orbado com fruta diez (Stir[?] a coral snake[?] with sweet potato), 233

Sorak (Saru salad), 346

Sweet potato (batata(s))...
Batata doce frite (Sweet sweet potato), 236

White marrow (...)
Caldeirão de abóbora branca (White pumpkin soup), 239

White tender (sot) tuos...
Bringala ribbat(g) White lentil with coconut, 222